THE CATHOLIC UNIVERSITY OF AMERICA
CANON LAW STUDIES
Number 97

# RESIDENCE OF PASTORS

## AN HISTORICAL SYNOPSIS AND COMMENTARY

A DISSERTATION

*Submitted to the Faculty of Canon Law of the Catholic University of America in partial Fulfillment of the requirements for the Degree of*

DOCTOR OF CANON LAW

BY

REV. PETER REILLY, J.C.L.
Priest of the Diocese of St. Augustine

THE CATHOLIC UNIVERSITY OF AMERICA
WASHINGTON, D. C.
1935

**Nihil Obstat:**

VALENTINUS T. SCHAAF, O.F.M., J.C.D.,
*Censor Deputatus.*

Washingtonii, D. C., die 27 Maii, 1935.

**Imprimatur:**

PATRITIUS BARRY, D.D.,
*Episcopus S. Augustini.*

S. Augustini, die 22 Maii, 1935.



Printed by
THE PAULIST PRESS
New York, N. Y.

TO THE BLESSED MOTHER

IN

REVERENCE AND GRATITUDE

## TABLE OF CONTENTS

PAGE

FOREWORD ........ vii

PART I

HISTORICAL SYNOPSIS

CHAPTER I

NOTION AND DIVISION OF RESIDENCE ........ 3

Article 1. Notion of Residence ........ 3

Article 2. Division of Residence ........ 4

CHAPTER II

DEVELOPMENT OF PASTOR'S RESIDENCE ........ 6

CHAPTER III

LEGISLATION FROM THE ELEVENTH CENTURY TILL THE COUNCIL OF TRENT ........ 9

CHAPTER IV

CAUSES EXCUSING FROM RESIDENCE ........ 11

CHAPTER V

LEGISLATION OF THE COUNCIL OF TRENT IN REGARD TO RESIDENCE ........ 14

Article 1. The Obligation of Residence ........ 14

Article 2. The Punishment for Its Non-Observance ........ 16

CHAPTER VI

PAGE

LEGISLATION AFTER THE COUNCIL OF TRENT ........ 20

CHAPTER VII

THE LAW BY WHICH PASTORS ARE BOUND TO RESIDENCE ........ 22

Conclusion ........ 27

PART II

CANONICAL EXPOSITION

CHAPTER VIII

COMMENTARY ON CANON 465 ........ 31

Article 1. The Pastor's Obligation to Residence ........ 31

Article 2. Residence in the Parochial House ........ 33

Article 3. Formal Residence ........ 35

Article 4. Residence Outside the Parochial House ... 36

CHAPTER IX

VACATIONS AND CAUSES FOR THEM ........ 38

Article 1. Formalities to be Observed During Absence ........ 38

Article 2. Christian Charity ........ 40

Article 3. Urgent Necessity ........ 40

Article 4. Due Obedience ........ 41

Article 5. Evident Utility to the Church or State 42

Article 6. Absence Over Two Months ........ 42

PAGE

Article 7. Power of the Substitute to Assist at Marriages ... 43

Article 8. Two Months' Absence ... 43

Article 9. Absence for More Than a Week ... 44

Article 10. Absence for Less Than a Week ... 45

Article 11. Computation of the Time of Absence ... 45

CHAPTER X

PROCEDURE AGAINST NON-RESIDENT PASTORS ... 48

Article 1. Procedure Against Pastors in General ... 48

Article 2. Procedure Against Irremovable Pastors ... 60

Article 3. Recourse Against Decree of Deprivation ... 64

Article 4. Transmission of the Acts ... 67

BIBLIOGRAPHY ... 69

ALPHABETICAL INDEX ... 73

BIBLIOGRAPHICAL SKETCH ... 75

CANON LAW STUDIES ... 77

# FOREWORD

THE obligation of pastors to reside has always been insisted on by Canon Law. The pastor is bound *ex officio* and *ex justitia* to exercise the care of souls over all his parishioners, who are not legitimately exempt.[1] Without any further law than this he would be bound to work on behalf of the souls committed to his care, but to insure that he carries out the duties imposed upon him, the Code adds another obligation in Canon 465, namely, the obligation of residing in his parish.

The precepts of the Code in regard to residence crystalize centuries of legislation, which is embodied in particular in the Decretals. There hardly any other statement occurs so often as the following: *"Nemo assumendus est nisi qui residere et curam per seipsum exercere valeat."* [2] This means that the pastor is bound to reside in his parish and to take the proper spiritual care of his parishioners.

The primary purpose of the present work is to give a clear idea of the pastor's obligation to residence, as contained in the Code. The obligation this legislation imposes is a fundamental one. If it is properly fulfilled most of the pastor's other duties are performed without difficulty; if it is neglected the faithful are sure to suffer as a consequence and many of the pastor's most important duties will be disregarded.

The dissertation is divided into two parts, the first giving a historical synopsis of the legislation on residence of pastors, and the second consisting of a commentary on the law of the present day.

The writer wishes at this point to express his profound gratitude to the Most Reverend Patrick Barry, D.D., Bishop of St. Augustine, for the opportunity of advanced studies in the field of Canon Law. The writer desires also to thank the members of the Faculty of the School of Canon Law for their kind and helpful direction and the many others who aided and encouraged in the preparation of this dissertation.

[1] Canon 464, § 1.

[2] *Cf.* c. 3, 4, X, *de clericis non residentibus,* III, 4.

# PART I

## HISTORICAL SYNOPSIS

# CHAPTER I

## NOTION AND DIVISION OF RESIDENCE

### Article 1. Notion of Residence

Residence in general means remaining or abiding where one's duties lie, or where one's occupation is properly carried on. Its primary purpose is that the duties imposed upon a person may be properly fulfilled. In Canon Law residence means more than mere abiding in a place and it may be defined as *"commoratio assidua et laboriosa, intra terminos loci quibus obedientiae aut muneris lege claudimur."*[1] To fulfill, therefore, the elements of the definition it must be accompanied by both work and vigilance. Mere living in a place, without the performance of the labors enjoined by one's state, is not the proper fulfillment of the precept of canonical residence. Hence residence differs from domicile, which is acquired by mere living in a place for the required period of time, or by the fact of settling down in a place with the intention of remaining there perpetually, *"si nihil inde avocet."*[2]

When a person is bound to residence he should not only always be morally present within the territory to which he is appointed, but he should carry out the duties his appointment entails. He should be morally present, *i. e.*, physical presence in the sense that he may never be absent is not required, because those who are absent for a short time and are soon to return are not considered absent.[3] Not only must he be morally present, but he must carry out the duties which his office imposes. He must personally serve the church to which he is appointed.[4] He must be present within the limits of the territory to which he is appointed. Thus a bishop is present if he resides within the limits of his diocese. A pastor resides within the limits of the territory given him if he lives within the boundaries of

[1] Maroto, *Institutiones Juris Canonici*, II, tit. III, c. 2.

[2] Canon 92.

[3] Schmalzgrueber, *Jus Ecclesiasticum Universum*, III, tit. IV, n. 4.

[4] Ferraris, *Bibliotheca*, VI, *"Residentia,"* n. 2.

his parish.[5] The Church has always been on her guard that only those clerics, who would reside and personally fulfill their obligations, be appointed to any office involving the care of souls.[6]

### Article 2. Division of Residence

Residence, in so far as the present work is concerned, may be divided into two main classes, namely, material and formal:

(a) By material residence is meant mere corporal presence or abiding in a place, without the execution of the proper office.[7] Such residence is of little avail in so far as Canon Law is concerned and it does not meet the requirements enjoined on those to whom the care of souls is committed. Canonical residence for those, to whom the care of souls is committed, is to be formal residence, *i. e.*, it is to be accompanied by work not by idleness.[8] Mere material residence is *otiosa* not *laboriosa* and the true idea of residence is not complied with, if one is present physically only and absent in mind, *i. e.*, by failure to carry out at least some of the duties of the office in which one is placed.

(b) Formal residence signifies that one is not only physically present but performs the duties, to which he is assigned.[9] It means that the person, to whom the care of souls is given, "preaches the word of God, gives good example, recalls the sheep that are straying from the fold, brings aid to those who are in distress and fights against the rapacious wolves, that in the clothing of sheep, seek to disturb and ensnare the members of the flock." [10]

Formal residence implies, therefore, vigilance and labor on the part of all those, who are entrusted with the care of souls. Those

[5] Schmalzgrueber, *Jus Ecclesiasticum Universum*, III, tit. IV, n. 2.

[6] *Cf.* c. 3, 4, X, *de clericis non residentibus*, III, 4. *"Talis ad hoc persona queretur quae residere in loco, et curam ejus per seipsum valeat exercere."*

[7] Wernz-Vidal, *Jus Canonicum*, II, p. 637.

[8] *Cf.* Bouix, *De Parocho*, p. 558; Sipos, *Juris Canonici*, p. 301.

[9] Wernz-Vidal, *Jus Canonicum*, II, p. 637.

[10] Benedict XIV, constitution, *Grave et permolestum*, August 15, 1741; *Benedicti XIV Bullarium*, I, XXVI.

who have the care of souls are not excused from their labors, even when they have assistants who are capable of carrying out the work. In such a case the pastor is still bound to his watchfulness and vigilance: he must at least carry out the principal duties of his office.[11]

[11] *Cf.* Benedict XIV, *De Synodo Dioecesana,* lib. XIII, c. XIX, n. 2; Smith, *Elements of Ecclesiastical Law,* I, 398.

## CHAPTER II

## DEVELOPMENT OF PASTOR'S RESIDENCE

In the early centuries of the Church there were no pastors as understood at the present day. In the strict sense bishops were the first pastors. Hence to obtain an idea of the law of residence in the first centuries it is necessary to consider the laws laid down for bishops.

The ancient name for an episcopal see for the first three hundred years was commonly "paroikia," which signified then the towns and villages near a city, which together with the city made up the diocese of the bishop.[1] There were not then any distinct parishes. The bishop exercised the care of souls over the whole diocese with the assistance of his priests, who were sent wherever the bishop wished, and were removable *"ad nutum episcopi."* To these priests were assigned means of sustenance which the bishop considered sufficient. The diocese formed one great parish.[2] About the fourth century country parishes began to be erected. It seems quite evident that no parishes as understood nowadays existed before that time.[3] In rural districts on account of the circumstances the development of parishes proceeded much more rapidly than in cities and there is no evidence for the existence of parishes in the cities, with the exception of Rome and Alexandria, before the tenth century.[4] The bishop's church was, during all this time, the only parish church in the city.[5] Hence in the first centuries of the Church the bishops were also the pastors and they are the ones to be considered when treating of the early laws in regard to residence of pastors.

[1] Bingham, *Origines Ecclesiasticae,* III, c. 2, I.

[2] Ferraris, *Bibliotheca,* VI, *Parochia,* n. 7.

[3] Bouix, *De Parocho,* p. 22; Wernz, *Jus Decretalium,* p. 689; Vecchiotti, *Institutiones Canonicae,* p. 328; Devoti, *Institutiones Canonicae,* I, tit. III, Sect. X, LXXXIX; Thomassin, *Vetus et Nova Ecclesiae Disciplina,* pars. I, lib. II, cap. XXII, pp. 3, 10.

[4] De Meester, *Jus Canonicum,* p. 244; Bouix, *De Parocho,* 23.

[5] Koudelka, *Pastors, Their Rights and Duties,* p. 9.

The enthusiasm and zeal of the bishops of the early centuries did not call for any criticism in the matter of the care of souls and the observance of residence. Those pastors of the early Church held in high esteem the dignity, to which they had been called, and their fervor and perseverance in their work were their outstanding characteristics.

The Council of Sardica (347) seems to have been the first to legislate in regard to residence. After discussing the evils that disregard of residence was sure to cause, the Council went on to determine various means by which the evils of non-residence were to be corrected. It seems that the bishops had begun to frequent the palaces of the Emperors. The Council determined that bishops should not do so unless they were first invited by the Emperor, or for the sake of helping those in necessity. To be absent they always required the permission of the Metropolitan and if he happened to be absent the permission of the Pope was required. Even if the cause of their absence was to help the poor and needy they were not to leave their diocese, if a deacon could carry out the work that was necessary. No bishop was allowed to delay in the diocese of another bishop and no bishop should be absent for more than three weeks without inevitable necessity.[6] The councils were not the only ones to lament the non-observance of residence in those early days. St. Cyprian also reproved bishops, who disregarded the divine commands, deserted their flocks and went into other dioceses in pursuit of worldly affairs.[7]

At the beginning of the sixth century, in the Council of Agatha, something new was added to the existing legislation. All clerics were forbidden to be absent from their churches on the more solemn feast days, namely, the Nativity, Epiphany, Easter and Pentecost.[8]

The Emperor Justinian during his reign in the sixth century also laid down some enactments in regard to residence. Patriarchs were bound to compel their bishops to remain in their own churches and they were not to be permitted to go away on long journeys.[9] Those

[6] Council of Sardica, Canons 8, 9, 10, 11, 12, 14, 15—Mansi, III, 25, 26, 27.

[7] St. Cyprian, *Liber de Lapsis*, § 6—*MPL*, IV, 470.

[8] Council of Agatha (506) Canon 64—Mansi, VIII, 336.

[9] Novel LXVII, c. 3.

bishops, who did not return to their own churches within the time specified by the sacred canons, were to be expelled from the episcopacy. Better men than they could be elected to fill their places.[10] Bishops, who through necessity, had to be absent from their dioceses, were not to leave without letters from their Patriarch or Metropolitan or the imperial permission.[11] It seems that the enactments of these early centuries had the desired effect in making bishops and all clerics feel the seriousness of their obligation and from the sixth to the tenth century very little legislation is to be found on the matter of residence. When abuses did spring up amongst the clergy, they were quickly checked by new decrees. The Council of Paris (829) reproved bishops because they delegated priests to carry on profane business, which could be done by others, with the result that infants died without baptism and penitents without confession.[12] The Capitularia of Charlemagne give an idea of the legislation of the ninth century. In one of his canons it is laid down that no priest should be allowed to say Mass in the parish of another, unless he was on a journey or had a good reputation in the parish.[13]

All through the early centuries, therefore, there existed a strict obligation to residence. Bishops and all clerics were bound to remain in their churches. Thomassin sums up the whole idea of the obligation in the following passage:

"Strictissima vero illa residendi necessitate constringuntur Abbates etiam, Parochique, quorum, ut et episcoporum, excusari non potest absentia, nisi vel necessitas inexorabilis, vel tam fructuosa compensatio, ut praesentiae eorum respondeat, tantoperae necessariae ad divinam Ecclesiae psalmodiam, ad verbi Dei praedicationem." [14]

[10] Novel CXXIII, c. 9.

[11] Novel CXXIII, c. 9.

[12] Canon 29—Mansi, XIV, 558.

[13] *Capitularium Collectio,* Canon 8—*MPL,* t. XCVII, p. 525.

[14] *Vetus et Nova Ecclesiae Disciplina,* pars. II, lib. III, c. XXXII, 2.

## CHAPTER III

## LEGISLATION FROM THE ELEVENTH CENTURY TILL THE COUNCIL OF TRENT

About the end of the eleventh century there existed many abuses in the Church. In their quest of riches and the glories of the world the clergy had become unmindful of their duties to God and the service they owed the churches committed to them. Hence it is not surprising to find in the Council of Nimes (1096) a decree to the effect that all priests, placed in churches to which the care of souls was attached, were to remain there for their whole life in the service of God. They were forbidden to move to richer churches. The penalty for disregard of this decree was loss of the church they already possessed and of the one which they attempted to acquire.[1] This legislation did not seem sufficient to put an end to the avarice of the clergy for again in the Third Lateran Council (1179), under the reign of Alexander III (1159-1181), it was found necessary to remind pastors and all others holding ecclesiastical benefices and dignities, that they were not to seek for the possession of many parishes and churches. Only those were to be chosen for the office of pastor who were willing to observe the law of residence and to exercise *per seipsos* the care of souls.[2] Innocent III (1198-1216), renewed in the Fourth Lateran Council (1215) all that had been decreed by Alexander III in the Third Council of the Lateran. No one, having a benefice with the care of souls attached, could obtain another such benefice. If anyone attempted to possess a second benefice having the care of souls he was to be deprived of both.[3] Those, who without a just and necessary cause deserted their parochial churches, were to be punished by privation, especially if

[1] Canon 9—Mansi, XX, 936.

[2] C. 3, X, *de clericis non residentibus,* III, 4.

[3] Canon 29—Mansi, XXII, 1015; c. 28, X, *de praebendis et dignitatibus,* III, 5.

they had gone away without the Patriarch's permission and after he had waited a sufficient time for them to return.[4]

To insure that the obligation of residence would be properly carried out each parish should have its own proper pastor.[5] Everyone appointed to a parochial church was bound to reside there personally so that the care of souls could be carried out diligently and faithfully.[6]

Particular synods also took up the work of reform and laws were passed to the effect that all pastors were to remain at their own churches.[7] Provisions were made by which priests were forbidden to be pastors of many churches and they were prohibited to absent themselves. Only men who were suitable were to be chosen.[8] From the time of these councils until the Council of Trent very little is found on the matter of residence. The Council of Trent, the great source of reform, took up the work of restoring once more the true idea of the obligation, which binds the pastor to remain with and to take care of the flock committed to him.

[4] Innocent III to the Patriarch of Constantinople, c. 10, X, *de clericis non residentibus*, III, 4.

[5] C. 30, X, *de praebendis et dignitatibus*, III, 5.

[6] C. 14, *de electione et electi potestate*, I, 6, in VI°.

[7] Council of Oxford (1222), Canon 14—Mansi, XXII, 1156.

[8] *Cf.* Council of London (1269), Canon 9—Mansi, XXIII, 1225; Council of Salisbury, Canon 10—Mansi, XXIV, 140.

## CHAPTER IV

## CAUSES EXCUSING FROM RESIDENCE

THOUGH the law of residence remained in force all through the centuries and was to be strictly observed by all, especially by those to whom the care of souls was committed, there always existed causes that excused from residence for a time. It is difficult to trace those causes in the early centuries, but there is sufficient evidence to say with certainty that they existed and that there occasionally arose circumstances justifying the absence of pastors from their churches. As early as the Council of Sardica (347) it can be gathered that bishops could frequent the palaces of the Emperors provided they had been invited by the Emperor.[1] Charity, too, seems to have formed an excusing cause for absence. St. Augustine relates that, for the sake of charity, he visited many provinces to spread the faith and his companions withdrew from their own churches and crossed the seas to spread the light of faith in other lands.[2] Obedience to the mandate of the Pope was also recognized as an excusing cause. During the first five centuries the Popes sent bishops as legates to the general councils of the East, or to the Patriarchs or the Emperors to settle rising heresies, to protect the faith, to purify morals and discipline, and to restore peace and concord amongst the people. The end was that good might redound to the whole Church.[3] Such, in general, were the causes that excused from residence in the early centuries. With the advance of time, causes for absence became a little more determined and more information is given as to when it was lawful to use them.

From the Council of Chalons (813),[4] which forbade pastors of souls, inferior to bishops, to go to Rome or Turin without the con-

[1] Canon 8—Mansi, III, 33.

[2] Epistle CXXII—*MPL,* XXXIII, 470.

[3] Thomassin, *Vetus et Nova Ecclesiae Disciplina,* pars. II, lib. III, c. XXXVI, n. 10.

[4] Canon 45—Mansi, XIV, 102.

sent of their bishops, it can be deduced that with their permission the pastors could absent themselves lawfully. Sometimes persecution, especially when it was directed against the person of the pastor and his presence would rather increase than mitigate it, excused the absence of the pastor.[5] St. Athanasius gives a similar example, when he fled because his life was threatened by Constantius, and his flight is justified by St. Augustine.[6] However, St. Augustine[7] says that this should not be the case when the danger is common to both the pastor and the flock committed to him. Then the pastor is bound to remain.[8] Temporary ill health was also considered as a sufficient excuse for absence for a time, when there was someone else available to take the place of the absent one.[9]

Study, as a cause for absence, is given much prominence in the Decretals. In the Third Lateran Council (1179) provisions were made for the better education of the clergy and to procure that the Council determined that there should be appointed in each Cathedral Church a teacher, who would instruct free of charge the clerics of that church. To provide for the necessities of the teacher a competent benefice was to be assigned to him.[10] During the reign of Alexander III (1159-1181), though absence of clerics for the sake of study was recognized as an excusing cause, the time of absence was not yet determined.[11] To Honorius III (1216-1227) belongs the credit of determining the period during which clerics could be absent to receive a better education. He permitted to clerics, who were students or professors, an absence of five years without any loss of the fruits of their benefices or praebends.[12] Pastors,

[5] *Cf.* St. Cyprian, Epistle XXXVI, *MPL,* IV, 326: "Oportet nos tamen paci communi consulere, quamvis cum taedio animi nostri deesse vobis, ne praesentia nostra invidiam et violentiam gentilium provocet, et simus auctores rumpendae pacis, qui magis quieti omnium consulere debemus."

[6] Epistle CCXXVIII, *MPL,* XXXIII, pp. 1015, 1016.

[7] St. Augustine, Epistle CCXXVIII—*MPL,* XXXIII, p. 1014.

[8] *Cf.* Benedict XIV, *De Synodo Dioecesana,* lib. XIII, c. XIX, q. 2.

[9] Thomassin, *Vetus et Nova Ecclesiae Disciplina,* pars. II, lib. III, c. LXVIII, n. 1.

[10] Canon 18—Mansi, XXII, 228.

[11] C. 4, X, *de clericis non residentibus,* III, 4.

[12] C. 5, X, *de magistris,* V, 5.

like other beneficaries, could avail themselves of this privilege, but found it difficult to do so, following the constitution of Gregory X (1271-1276) in the Second Council of Lyons (1274) where it was determined that anyone appointed to a parochial church was bound to reside there personally.[13] Boniface VIII (1294-1303) saw that this resulted in detriment to the Church by the lack of proper education among its pastors and by a new constitution he granted power to bishops to dispense pastors from residence for seven years' study. During these years of study the bishop was to provide for the care of souls by the deputation of a suitable vicar in the place of the absent pastor.[14] This privilege seems to have continued up to the time of the Council of Trent when it was abolished by the legisation laid down in the Council. The Fathers of the Council of Trent forbade absence for more than two months unless a grave cause for longer absence intervened. While study was admitted as a grave cause for absence before the Council, it could no longer remain such because of a prescription issued in Session XXIV, *de reformatione*, c. 18, by which a *concursus* was demanded for those to be appointed to the pastoral office. Such a *concursus* presupposed that the pastor was already suitable for his office and had already made the required studies. Consequently, it was no longer necessary for him to be absent for the sake of better education.[15] Barbosa [16] also refers to declarations of the Sacred Congregation of the Council issued on various occasions, to the effect that absence on account of study was no longer to be excused, as it had ceased to be a grave cause.

The Council of Trent itself did not elaborate much on causes for absence except to say that a grave one was necessary for a pastor whenever he was to be absent for more than two months. It mentioned as grave causes christian charity, urgent necessity, due obedience and evident utility to the Church or State.[17]

[13] C. *de electione et electi potestate,* I, 6, in VI°.

[14] C. 34, *de electione et electi potestate,* I, 6 in VI°.

[15] *Cf.* Bouix, *De Parocho,* p. 547; Henry, *De Residentia Beneficiatorum,* p. 204.

[16] *De Parocho,* pars. I, c. VIII, n. 27.

[17] Sess. XXIII, *de reformatione,* c. 1.

## CHAPTER V

## LEGISLATION OF THE COUNCIL OF TRENT IN REGARD TO RESIDENCE OF PASTORS

### Article 1. The Obligation of Residence

The care of souls was always looked upon as of the highest importance and the Council of Trent recognizing this set out diligently to reform the laxity of the clergy, so that those souls committed to their care might the more safely be guided to their eternal salvation. It began its reform with those who presided over the greater churches, "for" it said, "the integrity of those who govern is the safety of those who are governed." [1] It strengthened the residence of bishops by various sanctions, which included loss of one-fourth of the year's fruits for six months' illegal absence. For a further six months' absence loss of another fourth of the year's fruits was the penalty. If, after that, the non-resident still remained away from his diocese, the Metropolitan was bound to denounce him to the Holy See. If the Metropolitan himself happened to be unlawfully absent the oldest resident suffragan bishop should denounce him and the Holy See would then provide for the government of the diocese from which he absented himself.[2] In the case of other beneficiaries, inferior to bishops, the Council declared that all those in charge of any ecclesiastical benefice requiring personal residence should be compelled by their Ordinaries to observe the law of residence.[3] The Council forbade all perpetual dispensations from residence. Dispensations granted for a time, if they were examined and approved by the Ordinary were permitted. Whenever unlawful absence occurred, the bishop should provide for the care of souls by the deputation of a suitable vicar, who would receive due rewards from the fruits of the benefice.[4]

[1] Sess. VI, *de reformatione*, c. 1.
[2] Sess. VI, *de reformatione*, c. 1.
[3] Sess. VI, *de reformatione*, c. 2.
[4] Sess. VI, *de reformatione*, c. 2.

All the foregoing legislation was laid down at the beginning of the Council, but as some questioned the meaning of it, the Fathers found it necessary to lay down in unmistakable terms a new decree binding strictly all those to whom the care of souls belonged. The Council determined that all, who have the care of souls, are bound by divine precept to know their sheep and to offer sacrifice for them, to feed them by preaching of the divine word, by the administration of the sacraments and by good example, to have a paternal care for the sick and perform all the other pastoral obligations, all of which cannot be carried out by those who do not watch over their sheep, but desert them. Since all these duties cannot be performed by those who do not observe the law of residence, the Council determined that all to whom the care of souls is committed should be mindful of the divine precepts and should feed and guide their flocks in judgment and truth.[5]

Besides incurring the punishments laid down in Session VI, the non-resident was forbidden to partake of the fruits of his parish during his unlawful absence.[6] All these punishments extended to everyone with the care of souls.

"Eadem omnino, etiam quoad culpam et amissionem fructuum, et poenas, de curatis inferioribus et aliis quibuscumque, qui beneficium aliquod ecclesiasticum, curam animarum habens obtinet, sacrosancta synodus declarat et discernit."

The legislation laid down here was far reaching in its effects. It bound the pastor not only to material residence, but also commanded him to exercise the care of the souls of his parishioners by attending to their spiritual welfare, in which formal residence consists.

[5] Sess. XXIII, *de reformatione*, c. 1: "Cum praecepto divino mandatum sit omnibus quibus cura animarum commissa est, oves suas agnoscere, pro his sacrificium offere, verbique divini praedicatione, sacramentorum administratione, ac bonorum omnium operum exemplo pascere, pauperum, aliarumque miserabilium personarum curam paternam gerere, et in cetera munia pastoralia incumbere, quae omnia nequaquam ab iis praestari, et impleri possunt, qui gregi suo non invigilant, neque assistunt, sed mercenariorum more deserunt, sacrosancta synodus eos admonet et hortatur, ut divinorum praeceptorum memores, factique forma gregis in judicio et veritate pascant et regant."

[6] Sess. XXIII, *de reformatione*, c. 1.

The Council gave bishops power to appoint assistants to rectors in all parochial churches, where the people were so numerous that the pastor could not administer spiritually to them all.[7] This, however, did not excuse the pastor from his obligation of personal residence, because the pastor does not properly fulfill his duties if he leaves all the work of the parish to be done by his assistants.[8]

Provision for the pastor's vacation was made by allowing him an absence of two months annually. This absence could be extended for a grave cause. Certain means were determined by which no detriment to souls would follow on the absence. The cause of absence had to be made known to and approved by the Ordinary. If the Ordinary gave permission to be absent, he should do so in writing and free of charge. If the permission was refused by the Ordinary, the pastor could have recourse to the Metropolitan, who had power to compel the bishop to grant the permission, provided a just cause existed. While the absence lasted the pastor was bound to leave in his place a suitable vicar substitute, approved by the Ordinary.[9]

### Article 2. Punishment for Non-Observance of Residence

For non-residence the punishment throughout the ages was deprivation of the title or benefice, from which the cleric absented himself illegally.[10] The deprivation was carried out by means of a canonical trial. The Council of Nice (325) promulgated the law by which clerics should be subjected to a canonical trial before being deprived.[11] This was confirmed by the Council of Antioch (341) which demanded a canonical trial for the deprivation of a dignity or title.[12]

[7] Sess. XXI, *de reformatione,* c. 4.

[8] *Cf.* Reiffenstuel, *Jus Canonicum,* lib. III, tit. IV, n. 84; Benedict XIV, *De Synodo Dioecesana,* lib. XIII, c. XIX, § 2.

[9] Sess. XXIII, *de reformatione,* c. 1.

[10] *Cf.* Giraldus, *Expositio Juris Pontificii,* pars. I, ex lib. III, *Decretalium,* sect. CCCLIV: "Constans quidem semper fuit ejusdem ecclesiae vigilantia in eorumdem longiore punienda absentia cum privatione beneficii."

[11] Canon 5—Mansi, II, 670.

[12] Canons 11, 12—Mansi, II, 1314.

The councils of the eleventh and twelfth centuries bear witness to the fact that the practice of the Church was to deprive non-resident beneficiaries of their benefices by means of a canonical trial.[13]

Pope Celestine III (1191-1198) gives an example where a certain Dean, who was illegally absent, was first to be called and cited and then if he did not return his benefice was to be handed over to some one else.[14] This means of deprivation seems rather obscure. It fails to determine the time, within which the offender was bound to return. To the following Pope, Innocent III (1198-1216), belongs the credit of clearing up somewhat the existing difficulties about the form of procedure against non-residents. He determined that beneficiaries, who were not observing the law of residence, should not be deprived of their benefices unless, after they had been notified by the Ordinary, they failed to return within the time defined by him. This was the case where the non-resident could be personally cited.[15]

If, however, the non-resident could not be personally cited or if it was unknown where he was, then the process was different. In this case a threefold citation was to take place in the church of the benefice from which the beneficiary was absent. After the last of the three citations had taken place, the bishop should wait six months to give the absent beneficiary a chance to return. If he did not return within the six months, the bishop was to declare the benefice vacant.[16] The reason of the difference in the procedure was to find out if the offender was contumacious. In the case, where he could be personally cited and failed to return, it was easy to know whether he was contumacious or not. In the second case, namely, in regard to those, who could not be personally cited, there was a possibility that the citation would not reach them. Hence, arose the reason for

[13] *Cf.* Council of Nimes (1096), Canon 9—Mansi, XX, 936; Council of Clermont (1095), Canon 13—Mansi, XX, 817; Council of London (1125), Canon 9—Mansi, XXI, 332.

[14] *Cf.* c. 8, X, *de clericis non residentibus,* III, 4.

[15] C. 10, X, *de clericis non residentibus,* III, 4.

[16] *Cf.* c. 11, X, *de clericis non residentibus,* III, 4.

the delay of six months before declaring the benefice vacant. After the six months had elapsed there was a presumption of law that the citation had reached the non-resident.[17] Ten days interval between the three citations above mentioned was sufficient.[18]

This mode of procedure lasted up to the time of the Council of Trent. The Council, speaking of the procedure to be employed against non-resident pastors, ordained that, if after being cited, even if the citation was not personal, they remained contumacious, the Ordinary was free to proceed against them by ecclesiastical censure, sequestration, subtraction of the fruits and other remedies, even deprivation of their parish.[19]

The Council had already extended to pastors the same penalties for non-residence as it had determined for bishops offending in that respect. These penalties included, for more than three months' illegal absence, loss of the fruits or income in proportion to the time of absence.

Hence, the pastor, who violated the law of residence after the Council, incurred *ipso facto* loss of his income in proportion to the time of his illegal absence. This loss of the income cannot be considered as a true penalty in the sense that residence was a *conditio sine qua non* for its acquisition.[20] After the edict of citation was issued and was not complied with within the time therein laid down, the Ordinary could proceed to deprivation of the parish. Since the Council does not mention a threefold citation for those, who could not be personally cited, the one edict mentioned by the Council sufficed both for those who could be personally cited and for those, who for any reason could not be reached personally, and there was no necessity to delay six months in regard to the latter.[21] This means that the legislation laid down by the Council put an end to the three-

[17] *Cf.* Fagnanus, lib. III, *Decretalium,* c. 11, n. 12.

[18] Pirhing, *Jus Canonicum,* lib. III, sect. I, n. 58.

[19] Sess. XXIII, *de reformatione,* c. 1: "Quodsi, per edictum citati, etaim non personaliter, contumaces fuerint, liberum esse vult Ordinariis, per censuras ecclesiasticas, et sequestrationem, et subtractionem fructuum, aliamque juris remedia, etaim usque ad privationem compellere. . . . "

[20] *Cf.* Henry, *De Residentia Beneficiatorum,* p. 207.

[21] *Cf.* Fagnanus, lib. III, *Decretalium,* c. 11, n. 34.

fold citation issued to non-residents, who could not be personally cited, and to the personal citation in regard to those who could be reached personally. The Council used the words, "*per edictum citati, etiam non personaliter,*" without qualification. Hence whether a pastor could be cited personally or not, if he did not return to his parish within the time determined in the edict, he could be deprived of his parish without more ado.[22] While that seems to be the correct interpretation of the words of the Council there still were authors [23] who held that the procedure in existence before the Council still remained even after the Council. Hence, there remained doubt about the question till the Code finally settled it by its legislation on procedure against non-residents given in Canons 2381 and 2168-2176.[24]

[22] *Cf.* Henry, *De Residentia Beneficiatorum,* p. 211; Bouix, *De Parocho,* p. 570.

[23] Giraldus, *Expositio Juris Pontificii,* pars. I, lib. III; *Decretalium,* tit. IV, sect. CCCLIV; Barbosa, *De Parocho,* pars. I, c. VIII, n. 75; Garcias, *De Parocho,* pars. I, n. 75.

[24] *Cf.* Chelodi, *Jus de Personis,* p. 313, n. 4.

# CHAPTER VI

## LEGISLATION AFTER THE COUNCIL OF TRENT

After the Council of Trent very little legislation seems to have been enacted regarding the obligation of residence. This is due, perhaps, to far-reaching effects of the decrees of the Council, which bound so strictly all pastors to remain in their parishes.

In a few constitutions issued by the Popes there is sufficient evidence to show that the laws enacted in regard to residence still remained in force and bound the pastor just as strictly as ever. The first important warning to pastors as to their obligation of residence is found in the constitution *In Suprema* of Pius IV.[1] This constitution reminds all patriarchs, primates, archbishops, bishops, and all to whom the care of souls is committed of the laws laid down in the Council of Trent regarding residence. It seems abuses had developed because the Pope laments that pastors were disregarding their obligations with the result that loss of souls, bad example and scandal to many followed. He recalled to all again the fact that they were bound to personal residence by the same laws and under the same penalties as were determined in the Council.

The constitution, *Cupientes,* of Pius V [2] seems to have been intended to put an end to another abuse, namely, the negligence of pastors to reside at their parochial churches. The constitution commands all pastors to reside in their parochial churches and to carry out their divine services there. To enforce these obligations bishops could put the offending pastors under pecuniary fines and censures and could even go so far as to inflict deprivation of the parish on the negligent pastor.

In the constitution, *Ad Militantis,*[3] Benedict XIV pointed out that all the censures, sequestration and subtraction of the fruits and other provisions for compelling pastors to residence, in accordance

[1] 25 November, 1564—*Fontes,* n. 109.

[2] 8 July, 1568—*Fontes,* n. 127.

[3] 30 March, 1742—*Fontes,* n. 326.

with the decrees of the Council of Trent, still remained in force. Two years later the same Pope placed on the bishop the obligation of enquiring, during his episcopal visitation, as to whether each pastor had observed the law of residence in the past and whether at the present time he was faithful in his duties in regard to it.[4] These documents of the Popes are evidence of their solicitude that the law of residence be observed. They point out that the legislation enacted by the Council of Trent, the great reformer in the matter of residence, was not to be disregarded but on the contrary bound as strictly as the terms of the legislation indicate.

[4] *Cf. Constitution, Firmandis,* 6 March, 1744, § 9—*Fontes,* n. 349.

## CHAPTER VII

## THE LAW BY WHICH PASTORS ARE BOUND TO RESIDENCE

It has never been defined that pastors and others with the care of souls are bound to residence from divine law, so that the matter still remains a subject of controversy amongst canonists. For centuries the question had never arisen, because all without exception considered that pastors of souls were bound by divine law to observe their obligation to residence. According to Fagnanus,[1] Ambrosius Catherinus was the first to question this. Before the decrees on residence were issued in the Council of Trent, the question was debated at length amongst the Fathers of the Council.[2] The result of the debate was that the Fathers refrained from defining the matter and it remains a question open to discussion. The practical outcome of the dispute among the Fathers of the Council was a new decree condemning non-observance of residence.

As most of the argumentation regarding the question to be dealt with in this chapter centers around this decree of the Council it is well to repeat it here. Afterwards the opinions on both sides shall be given.

"Cum praecepto divino mandatum sit omnibus quibus cura animarum commissa est, oves suas agnoscere, pro his sacrificium offere, verbique divini predicatione, sacramentorum administratione, ac bonorum omnium operum exemplo pascere, pauperum aliarumque miserabilium personarum curam paternam gerere, et in cetera munia pastoralia incumbere, quae omnia nequaquam ab iis praestari, et impleri possunt, qui gregi suo non invigilant, neque assistunt, sed mer cenariorum more deserunt, sacrosancta synodus eos admonet et hortatur, ut divinorum praeceptorum memores, factique forma gregis in judicio et veritate pascant et regant." [3]

[1] Lib. III, *Decretalium*, c. VIII, *de clericis non residentibus*, nn. 20, 21.

[2] *Cf.* Benedict XIV, *De Synodo Dioecesana*, lib. VII, § 1, n. 3; Chelodi, *Jus de Personis*, p. 313.

[3] Sess. XXIII, *de reformatione*, c. 1.

Here it is evident the Council refrained from defining that residence of pastors is of divine precept. If the Council wished to issue such a definition, it would have said so in unmistakable terms as was the custom of the Fathers in drawing up definitions on matters of divine and Catholic faith. It can be also noted that the above decree is placed, not amongst the definitions pertaining to dogma, but amongst the decrees *de reformatione*. It is true too that the Church has never condemned anyone, who pertinaciously denied that the precept of residence for pastors is merely of ecclesiastical law. The Church would have acted quite otherwise if this were a matter to be held as an article of faith.

The question, then, is residence of pastors and others with the care of souls of divine precept or not? The principal arguments of those who deny that the obligation is of divine law may be summed us as follow:

(1) They say that while it cannot be denied that all the duties mentioned in the first part of the decree of the Council are based on divine precept, it does not, however, follow that to fulfill these duties the pastor must reside under divine precept. If that were necessary these duties would have to be carried out by the pastor personally and could not be delegated to anyone else, but it often happens that all or at least some of these duties, such as preaching and the administration of the sacraments are *de facto* delegated.

(2) They say that the presence of the pastor is not necessary for the giving of good example or the offering of sacrifice for the members of the parish. This, they say, is evident from the words of the Council, "*quae omnia nequaquam ab iis praestari et impleri possunt, qui gregi suo non invigilant neque assistunt sed mercenariorum more deserunt.*" The Council did not say that the duties it inculcated could not be fulfilled by those who are *absent*, but by those who "*non invigilant neque assistunt.*" According to Benedict XIV [4] the words "*non invigilant neque assistunt*" can be referred to the mind, since a pastor can be said to exercise vigilance and assistance towards his flock, even when he is absent physically, if in mind he is watchful over their interests.

[4] *De Synodo Dioecesana*, lib. VII, c. I, § 4.

(3) The end for which residence of pastor is imposed is the spiritual welfare of souls. It becomes lawful for the pastor to be absent if he can attain the end of the law during his absence. If a pastor, who is present physically and absent in mind by the fact that he does not exercise the care of souls, does not fulfill the precept of residence, so, too, on the contrary, the pastor, who is absent physically, can fulfill the obligation of residence if in mind he is vigilant over the interests of his parishioners.[5]

(4) Finally those opposed to the teaching that residence of pastors is of divine precept, say that there is no text of Sacred Scripture on which the precept could be based.

Despite those arguments, the opinion which maintains that residence of pastors is based, at least fundamentally, on divine precept seems very probable and is based on the following general arguments:

(1) Bishops, pastors and all to whom the care of souls is committed are bound by divine precept to know their sheep, to preach to them, to administer the sacraments to them, and to carry out the other duties mentioned in the early part of the decree on residence issued by the Council of Trent. Furthermore, the Council said that all these duties cannot be carried out by those who do not watch over and stand by (*assistunt*) their flocks but on the contrary desert them after the manner of mercenaries. Hence it seems to follow that fundamentally the obligation to reside is also placed by divine precept on all to whom the care of souls is given.[6]

(2) By the same law as one is bound to an end, he is bound to the means to attain that end. The means the pastor is bound to employ in his office as shepherd over his flock are founded in divine precept. These means he cannot properly fulfill unless he resides with his parishioners. His presence is demanded if he wishes to know his parishioners, to administer to their spiritual needs, to preach to them, to exercise vigilance over them and to have a paternal care for them. All these duties are founded on divine command. Hence the

[5] *Cf.* Henry, *De Residentia Beneficiatorum,* pp. 21, 22; Benedict XIV, *De Synodo Dioecesana,* lib. VII, c. I, § 4.

[6] *Cf.* Fagnanus, lib. III, *decretalium, de clericis non residentibus,* c. VIII, n. 29.

obligation of personal residence, without which the pastor cannot fulfill these duties, seems to be based on divine command.

(3) While it is true that there is no text of Sacred Scripture to prove directly the obligation of residence, still the obligation seems to follow at least indirectly from such texts as the following: "Take heed to yourselves and the whole flock wherein the Holy Ghost hath placed you bishops, to rule the Church of God, which He hath purchased with His own Blood." [7] "Be thou vigilant, labour in all things, do the work of an evangelist, fulfil thy ministry." [8] The pastor seems to come under these injunctions of Sacred Scripture. He is the one placed over the flock in his parish to know them and to minister to them, to do the work of an evangelist among them. It is difficult to see how he can fulfill these duties unless by the observance of personal residence.

"Feed the flock of God which is among you, taking care of it, not by constraint, but willingly, according to God." [9] Cornelius à Lapidé, commenting on this passage, says that by it bishops and pastors are bound to watch over their flocks and in every way to provide for them. Wherefore he says that they are bound to reside with their flock and to visit it often. Then he draws the conclusion that residence is imposed on bishops and pastors by both human and divine precept.[10] Again "he that entereth in by the door is the shepherd of the sheep and they hear his voice: and he calleth his own sheep by name . . . and he goeth before them and the sheep follow him, bcause they know his voice. But a stranger they follow not but fly from him, because they know not the voice of strangers." [11] These words demonstrate the office and the duty of the pastor. They indicate that there is placed on him a personal evangelical precept to be a leader and a spiritual guide to his parishioners. If he deserts them after

[7] Acts XX, 28.

[8] Timothy IV, 5.

[9] 2 Peter V, 2.

[10] Cornelius à Lapidé, *Commentarium in Sacram Scripturam,* XIX, p. 414, 415: "Quocirca apud eum residere, eumque crebro obire et visitare debent. Hinc residentia Episcopis et Pastoribus praecepta est jure humano et divino."

[11] John X, 2-5.

the manner of a hireling he cannot be their guide, he cannot know them and they cannot know his voice.

It may be argued that the pastor can fulfill his duties, in regard to residence, by delegating some one to carry them out in his place. Delegation does not conform to the requirements laid down in the Decretals for all those, who were chosen to be pastors.[12] It may also be said that since the office of pastor is not of divine institution, his obligation to reside is not of divine precept. While it is true that the office of pastor is not of divine institution, it is also true that the duties encumbent on him are of divine institution, *e. g.*, administration of the sacraments, teaching and preaching. He cannot carry out these duties unless he resides personally with his parishioners. Hence, it seems true to say that fundamentally his obligation to residence is of divine precept.

Furthermore almost all authors agree that the obligation of residence for the pastor arises from divine law.[13] The view they hold seems to be the correct one. Christ Himself as the exemplar of the perfect pastor and indirectly by His teaching on the duties of the good shepherd to know his sheep seems to indicate that a pastor to fulfill properly his duties as a shepherd must be present with his flock. He Himself remained with His followers day in and day out during His public life. He, therefore, set an example to all pastors of souls. By His example, at least, He taught pastors the lesson that they must remain and abide with their parishioners.

While it is true that the pastor may for a time commit to his assistants or to other priests some or all the duties of his office, he is not the true pastor if he does so continually. He is not following the example of Christ, nor is he following His command to be vigilant, to labor in all things and to fulfill his ministry, which is committed to him.

[12] C. 3, 4, X, de clericis non residentibus, III, 4: "Nemo assumendus est nisi qui residere et curam per seipsum exercere valeat."

[13] *Cf.* Henry, *De Residentia Beneficiatorum*, p. 23; St. Alphonse, *Theologia Moralis*, IV, p. 40; Benedict XIV, *De Synodo Dioecesana*, lib. VII, c. I, § 6; Cocchi, *De Personis*, p. 418; Fagnanus, lib. III, *decretalium, de clericis non residentibus*, c. VIII, n. 25 et sq.; Chelodi, *Jus de Personis*, p. 314; Deshayes, *Memento Juris Ecclesiastici*, p. 240; Bouuaert, *Manuale Juris Canonici*, p. 137.

While it is not defined by the Church that the obligation of the pastor to reside is of divine law the weight of opinion is in favor of its being of divine precept and Christ's example and teaching seem to point in the same direction.

## Conclusion

A few general remarks here will be sufficient to give an idea of the attitude of the Church in regard to the residence of pastors throughout the centuries.

The Church from the beginning looked upon the care of souls as of the utmost importance. She realized that the pastor, on whom the care of souls is placed, cannot properly carry out this care unless he is ever present with his flock and ready to attend to their needs and to minister to them in their spiritual affairs. Hence it is not surprising that in the beginning the Church enforced the law of residence and was never slow to correct abuses when they arose in regard to it. In the early centuries, though the evidence is scarce, there is sufficient proof that the pastor of souls had an important duty to perform, a duty which he could not fulfill properly unless he resided personally in his parish. The Popes in General Councils and the bishops in particular synods were ever watchful that this obligation of the pastor was carried out with fidelity.

During the reigns of Alexander III, Innocent III and the other Popes of that time the duty of residence became more clearly manifest. Causes permitting lawful absence and penalties for illegal absence were more clearly defined. The decrees of the Council of Trent were the most far-reaching of all. They determined in particular the penalties for non-observance of residence. They did not, however, define that the obligation of the pastor to personal residence arises from divine law, so that the question remains open for discussion amongst canonists.

The present-day legislation on the pastor's obligation to residence will be considered in detail in the following chapters of this work.

# PART II

## CANONICAL EXPOSITION

## CHAPTER VIII

## COMMENTARY ON CANON 465

### Article 1. Obligation of Pastor to Reside

In this chapter a summary of the obligation of the pastor to both formal and material residence, will be given. The nature of the pastor's office binds him to both. He must be present with his parishioners and not only must he be present but he must also exercise the care of souls to which he is appointed. The pastor is, as it were, a shepherd to the souls committed to his care and like the shepherd, who ever remains with his sheep and watches over them, the pastor must be ever on his guard against detriment to the spiritual welfare of the souls, whose guardian and shepherd he is.

> **Canon 465, § 1: Parochus obligatione tenetur residendi in domo paroeciali prope suam ecclesiam; loci tamen Ordinarius potest iusta de causa permittere ut alibi commoretur, dummodo domus ab ecclesia paroeciali non ita distet ut paroecialium perfunctio munerum aliquid inde detrimenti capiat.**

Under the obligations laid down in the present canon will come both removable and irremovable pastors, quasi pastors, vicarii oeconomii, *i. e.,* those who take charge of a parish while it is vacant,[1] substitute vicars, *i. e.,* those who take charge of a parish during absence of the pastor, or those who are appointed to take care of a parish of a pastor who has been removed and is having recourse to the Holy See[2] and assistants endowed with full parochial power,[3] *e. g.,* those appointed to a pastor, who through old age or permanent infirmity is unable to carry out the pastoral duties. Since all the

[1] *Cf.* Canon 472, § 1.

[2] *Cf.* Canon 474.

[3] *Cf.* Canon 475.

above mentioned persons enjoy all the privileges and are bound to the same duties as all pastors of souls, it follows that they are also bound to observe the law of residence.[4]

The obligation of the pastor to observe the law of residence arises from the fact that he is obliged to exercise the care of souls over all his parisioners.[5] The Church, realizing that the care of souls cannot be properly carried out, unless the person, burdened with such an obligation, is present and ready to undertake the due vigilance and direction of those souls, wisely lays down the duty of residence for the pastor, who is the shepherd appointed to feed and nourish the flock in his parish. Hence, it is not surprising to find that the Church was always most solicitous that pastors should be present in their churches and should exercise personally the care of souls. From the beginning this obligation was insisted upon and in the Decretals especially there is ample proof of the anxiety of the Church that only men who were able to take care of the flock in the proper manner be appointed pastors. Few statements appear so often as the following: *"Nemo assumendus est nisi qui residere et curam per seipsum exercere valeat."* [6] This was the Church's idea of residence all through the ages. The Council of Trent made it clear that the pastor's obligation in this regard is a grave one. After the Council had declared that bishops were bound *sub gravi* to residence, it went on to state that pastors and all others with the care of souls were bound in the very same manner.[7] Hence, there cannot be any doubt about the seriousness of the obligation of residence imposed upon a pastor when he is appointed to a parish. His obligation to remain in his parish with his flock is a grave one.[8] There are various ways in which the pastor may sin against this obligation. He might violate it by detriment caused to the flock in case he went away and left no priest in his place or made no provision for the presence of a priest, who would attend the sick or dying. His guilt

[4] *Cf.* Cocchi, *De Personis,* pars. I, p. 399; Smith, *Elements of Ecclesiastical Law,* I, p. 398.

[5] *Cf.* Canon 464, § 1.

[6] *Cf.* c. 3, 4, X, *de clericis non residentibus,* III, 4.

[7] Sess. XXIII, *de reformatione,* c. 1.

[8] St. Alphonse, *Theologia Moralis,* IV, p. 40.

might also arise from prolonged absences extending beyond the time allowed by the Code, *e. g.*, if he were to remain away more than two months annually without a grave cause, or he could be guilty of violation of his obligation to residence if he leaves the parish for extended periods without the required permission, *e. g.*, if he went away for two or three weeks without the bishop's leave, or if he were absent for even a shorter time when permission had been expressly denied. This would be especially true if, despite the bishop's refusal to grant permission, he went away without any cause at all or were absent on the more solemn feast days.[9] Hence, there are many and varied ways by which the pastor's duty of residence may be neglected and even violated. In the consideration of the regular vacation allowed the pastor, the various causes that excuse absence will be dealt with in detail.

So far the general obligation of the pastor to reside in the parish has been treated. Not only is he bound to reside in the parish but he is also obliged to live in the parish house.

## Article 2. Residence in the Parish House

The parish church is considered by all the parishioners as the place where they may find the pastor when they need his spiritual ministrations and his counsel. This seems to be the mind of the legislator in determining that the pastor is bound to reside at the parish church. This was the law in the past, though perhaps it was not so clearly defined as it is today. The pastor was expected to be present at his church, so that he might exercise more diligently the care of souls.[10] The present-day legislation on the pastor's obligation to be present at the parochial church is clear. He is to be present there continuously; there he is to reside night and day.[11] However, it can be gathered from replies of the Sacred Congregation of the Council that the pastor does not incur the penalties for non-

[9] *Cf.* De Meester, *Juris Canonici*, p. 293.

[10] *Cf.* c. 14, *de electione et electi potestate*, I, 6, in VI°; Fagnanus, lib. III, *Decretalium*, c. *"Extirpandae," "Qui Vero,"* de praebendis, n. 12.

[11] *Cf.* Fagnanus, *De Jure Parochorum*, p. 125; Pius V, constitution, *Cupientes*, 8 July, 1568—*Fontes*, n. 127.

residence, provided he lives within the parish limits, even if his residence is not in the parish house.[12]

Of course, it is not to be expected that he is bound so strictly that he may never leave the house. His abiding in the parochial house is not to be interpreted so that he would be bound to be physically present there every minute of the day. Moral presence is all that is required, *i. e.*, for a just cause he may be absent for a short time,[13] because those who are absent for a short time and are soon to return are not considered absent.[14] Hence, he would be allowed his daily hour or two of recreation to keep him in fit physical condition for the labors of his office. Two or three hours' absence every day seems to be quite justifiable, as nobody can be expected to spend a life confined to a house night and day.[15] Even longer absences than two or three hours seem to be excused provided they do not occur habitually. Occasions will arise in every pastor's life calling for his attendance at certain functions, such as funerals and Solemn Masses. On such occasions when the ordinary rules of friendship and courtesy call for the attendance of the pastor, he has sufficient excuse for absence long enough to allow attendance.[16] To provide against the dangers that might arise during such absences he should leave word at his home as to his whereabouts and with the conveniences afforded by the use of the automobile and telephone at the present day he will be easily found in a short time to attend to any sudden call.

The opinion of Vermeersch,[17] which indicates that a few hours' absence every day would violate the obligation of residence, seems to be too strict because of the statement of the Council of Trent [18] that those who are absent for a short time and are soon to return are not to be considered absent and because of the fact that the

[12] S. C. C., 26 November, 1864—*A. S. S.*, II, 285, et seq.

[13] De Meester, *Juris Canonici*, p. 289.

[14] *Cf.* Concilium Trid., sess. XXIII, *de reformatione*, c. 1; De Meester, *Juris Canonici*, p. 289.

[15] *Cf.* Cocchi, *De Personis*, p. 420; De Meester, *Juris Canonici*, p. 290.

[16] *Cf.* De Meester, *Juris Canonici*, p. 290; Coronata, *Institutiones Juris Canonici*, III, p. 533.

[17] *Epitome Juris Canonici*, p. 401.

[18] Sess. XXIII, *de ref.*, c. 1.

office of the pastor, who carries out his duties properly, is one filled with many worries and cares that demand a little relaxation daily. Moreover the pastor seems to be reasonably present to answer the calls of his parishioners, if he is present twenty out of the twenty-four hours of the day. As a matter of fact, absence of a day or two each week seems quite justified. The Council of Portland in Oregon allows pastors to be absent for one or, if necessary, two days during the week for the sake of recreation.[19] It seems that this absence of a day or two each week does not count as part of the regular vacation, since the pastor, who needs recreation, will usually leave home in the morning and arrive back in the afternoon or evening.

As no author has dealt with this question, the writer leans towards the opinion that this one or two days' absence does not form part of the annual vacation. The pastor must of course fulfill his regular duties and should leave word during his absence as to where he may be found in case an urgent call arises.

## Artice 3. Formal Residence

The pastor's obligation to residence does not cease with mere abiding in the parish. More than material residence is required before the obligation is properly fulfilled. The pastor is bound not only to reside, but to work on behalf on the flock committed to him. That was a condition requisite in pastors for centuries. Only those men were to be chosen for the pastor's office who were willing not only to reside, but also to exercise personally the care of souls.[20] The law of residence for a pastor is not to be understood of material residence only but also of formal residence, that is residence joined with work not with idleness,[21] because residence is understood to mean something *laboriosa,* not *otiosa.*[22] The pastor is, therefore, bound to work on behalf of his parishioners. The fact that he has

[19] *Cf. Acta et Decreta Concilii Provincialis Portlandensis in Oregon Quarti,* n. 130.

[20] *Cf.* c. 3, 4, X, *de clericis non residentibus,* III, 4.

[21] Bouix, *De Parocho,* 558.

[22] Schmalzgrueber, *Jus Ecclesiasticum Universum,* III, tit. IV, n. 4; Oesterle, *Praelectiones Juris Canonici,* I, 217; Sipos, *Juris Canonici,* p. 301.

assistants, who are capable of undertaking all the parish work, does not excuse him from performing his share of the duties that arise. By observing material residence only he violates the obligation imposed upon him and according to authors is guilty of sin, if he leaves all the work of the parish to his curates.[23] Of course, if he has assistants it is not to be expected that he will undertake the more arduous duties of the parish, such as attendance to night calls and outlying missions. The pastor is generally a man who has borne the burden and heat of the day, and it is not to be demanded that, when he has assistants, he should attend to the more difficult duties; but he must not cease to employ himself in the ordinary parochial duties, such as preaching, the hearing of confessions and the administration of the other sacraments, and in answering the reasonable calls of his parishioners when they ask for him personally.[24] The pastor is, therefore, obliged to perform the ordinary duties arising in every parish. He may leave the more difficult ones to his assistants.[25] Mere supervision of the work of the parish by the pastor does not fulfill the requirements of formal residence. This seems clear from the Decretals, which demanded that only those men should be selected for the pastor's office, who were able to exercise personally the care of souls.[26] All the above-mentioned authors hold that the pastor is bound to carry out his share of the ordinary parochial duties, even when he has assistants.

### Article 4. Residence Outside the Parochial House

The Ordinary can for a just cause permit the pastor to reside outside the parish house, provided the house he chooses to live in is not so far removed from the parish church that the attendance to the duties of the parish will suffer as a consequence. Not every

[23] Cocchi, *De Personis*, p. 419; Fanfani, *De Jure Parochorum*, p. 125; Smith, *Elements of Ecclesiastical Law*, p. 398; Sipos, *Juris Canonici*, p. 301.

[24] Bargilliat, *Praelectiones Juris Canonici*, p. 153; Bouuaert, *Manuale Juris Canonici*, p. 317; S. C. C., 10 March, 1742—Richter, *Canones et Decreta Co. Trid.*, p. 39, n. 20.

[25] Smith, *Elements of Ecclesiastical Law*, I, p. 398; Augustine, *Commentary*, p. 549.

[26] C. 3, 4, X, *de clericis non residentibus*, III, 4.

cause will suffice for the granting of such permission. The fact that the pastor has assistants, who are present at the church and are capable of carrying out all the parochial duties, does not form a sufficient excuse to permit the pastor to reside elsewhere.[27] The personal character of the pastor's duties, which oblige him to the care of souls demands his personal presence at the church, to which he is appointed rector, and permission to live away from there should be granted reluctantly. It is unlawful for the pastor to reside outside the parish house, even within the limits of the parish, without a just cause and the permission of the Ordinary. He could be fined for such conduct and compelled to return.[28] When the pastor has no parochial house, a different question presents itself. In this case he will have to make provision to reside at least within the limits of the parish and as near as possible to the parish church.[29] This can be done by renting a house in the vicinity of the church. When this is not feasible, as may sometimes happen, owing to the impossibility of finding a proper home, it seems the Ordinary could allow the pastor to live outside the parish for a time, in some place as convenient as possible to the church.[30]

[27] *Cf.* S. C. C., 10 May, 1687—Richter, *Canones et Decreta Concilii Tridentini*, p. 38, n. 11; S. C. C., 1589—*A. S. S.*, XII (1879), p. 362.

[28] *Cf.* Zitelli, *Apparatus Juris Canonici*, p. 175.

[29] *Cf.* S. C. C., 6 April, 1606—*A. S. S.*, XII (1879), p. 362.

[30] *Cf.* S. C. C., 3 June, 1592—Pallottini, *Collectio Resolutionum*, S. C. C., t. 14, *Parochus*, art. XII, n. 44; De Meester, *Juris Canonici*, p. 289; Bouix, *De Parocho*, p. 561; Coronata, *Juris Canonici*, I, p. 565.

# CHAPTER IX

## VACATIONS AND CAUSES FOR THEM

### ARTICLE 1. FORMALITIES TO BE OBSERVED DURING ABSENCE

THE law of residence is not to be understood in the sense that the pastor may never for a just cause be absent from his parish. The legislation before the Code always recognized causes for absence and excused it when it did not extend beyond the limits permitted by the law. The canon to be dealt with now determines the length of the vacation the pastor is allowed, the permission required for the vacation and the various other conditions to be fulfilled in order to comply with the present-day legislation on the matter of residence of pastors.

**Canon 465, § 2. Eidem abesse permittitur per duos ad summum intra annum menses sive continuos sive intermissos, nisi gravis causa, judicio ipsius Ordinarii, vel diuturniorem absentiam requirat vel breviorem tantum permittat.**

**§ 3. Dies quibus parochus piis exercitiis vacat ad normam can. 126, non computantur, semel in anno, in duobus vacationum mensibus, de quibus in § 2.**

**§ 4. Sive continuum sive intermissum sit vacationum tempus, cum absentia ultra hebdomadam est duratura, parochus, praeter legitimam causam, habere debet Ordinarii scriptam licentiam et vicarium substitutum sui loco relinquere ab eodem Ordinario probandum; quod si parochus sit religiosus, indiget praeterea consensu Superioris et substitutus tum ab Ordinario tum a Superiore probari debet.**

**§ 5. Si parochus repentina et gravi de causa discedere atque ultra hebdomadam cogatur abesse, quamprimum per litteras Ordinarium commonefaciat, ei indicans causam discessus et sacerdotem supplentem, eiusque stet mandatis.**

**§ 6. Etiam pro tempore brevioris absentiae parochus debet fidelium necessitatibus providere, maxime si id peculiaria rerum adjuncta postulent.**

In this canon the formalities to be observed when it is necessary to be absent are determined in brief. The pastor is allowed two months' absence annually, to be taken intermittently or at one time as the case may be. While the Code does not mention that a cause is necessary for this vacation of two months it is certain that a cause of some kind is necessary. That the cause required need not be grave can be gathered from the fact the law specifies that a grave cause be present when a vacation longer than two months is to be taken, because by the demanding of a grave cause for an absence of over two months the canon equivalently states that an absence which does not extend over two months does not require a grave cause.[1]

Four hypotheses may arise in dealing with the question of vacations:

(a) Absence of more than two months. This cannot be granted unless for a grave cause.

(b) Absence of two months, which a reasonable cause seems to justify.

(c) Absence for over a week, and

(d) Absence for a few days or less than a week.

These four cases of absence will be treated in order. For every absence of over two months the pastor requires, besides the consent of the Ordinary, a grave cause. To determine what is really a grave cause as understood here is a difficult matter and to obtain some light on the subject one must turn to the legislation before the Code. A grave cause as determined by the Council of Trent[2] can come under one of four headings, namely, Christian charity, urgent necessity, due obedience and evident utility to the Church or State.

[1] *Cf.* Bouix, *De Parocho,* p. 542.

[2] Session XXIII, *de reformatione,* c. 1.

### Article 2. Christian Charity

The first grave cause, Christian charity, will include such excuses as the mission of a pastor to settle serious disputes, absence to aid a church in distress or to convert to the faith a fallen away province or parish, to help parents and benefactors.[3] Hence a pastor may be allowed an absence of more than two months if circumstances arise calling for his intervention in serious cases of dispute or distress. It is always to be understood, however, that his absence does not cause serious detriment to his own parishioners. In such a case his absence would be contrary to charity and instead of leaving his parish he would be bound to remain at home. The care of souls, to which he is appointed in his own parish, is his primary duty; to it he must devote himself diligently and zealously and when there is danger that he will violate that charge seriously by his absence, even if the absence is intended to be of help to some one else, he is not permitted to leave his own flock.

### Article 3. Urgent Necessity

Under this heading will come such causes as danger of death from his enemies, grave loss of temporal goods, war, persecution, or danger from an enemy, serious ill health, poverty and distress. In all these cases too it is necessary that the presence of the pastor is not required for the salvation of the souls of those committed to his care. Besides it is required that the danger to the pastor is personal. When it is common danger affecting both pastor and people he must remain with them.[4] He is the shepherd of the flock over which he is appointed and "the good shepherd giveth his life for his sheep." [5] In this respect a grave cause could also arise from such sources as inclemency of the weather, gout, rheumatism, serious ill-health, *e. g.*, if a pastor is ill in a parish, where on account of lack of good doctors, he cannot receive proper treatment. In such a

[3] *Cf.* Henry, *De Residentia Beneficiatorum*, p. 190.

[4] *Cf.* Benedict XIV, *De Synodo Dioecesana*, lib. XIII, c. XIX, § 2; Henry, D *Residentia Beneficiatorum*, p. 191.

[5] John X, 11.

case he could be permitted to be absent long enough to receive the necessary medical attention.[6] The outbreak of an epidemic such as smallpox, yellow fever and influenza does not seem to be a sufficiently grave excuse to justify absence, because in such cases the danger is common to both the pastor and his parishioners.[7] If a pastor becomes so impoverished that he finds it necessary to leave his parish to seek financial aid elsewhere it seems the bishop could permit, in such a case, an absence longer than the absence usually allowed.[8]

### Article 4. Due Obedience

The pastor may be permitted an absence extending over two months, when the cause of his absence is obedience to the mandate of the Pope or his own bishop. The Pope, on account of his supreme power, may, of course, employ a pastor in any negotiation or business that he thinks necessary, but the same does not seem to hold true of the bishop's employment of the pastor. From replies of the Sacred Congregation of the Council cited by Barbosa,[9] it seems that the bishop is not free to commit to the pastor any office requiring absence from his parish for more than the two months' annual vacation. Hence, it is hardly in accordance with Canon Law if a pastor is employed as chancellor, secretary, or in any other capacity requiring most of his time and attention. The holding of such a position naturally means that the pastor cannot possibly devote himself to the duties of his parish with the fidelity and zeal demanded of all those, to whom the care of souls is committed.[10] A pastor employed as chancellor, while he may be able to comply with the demands of material residence, certainly cannot fulfill his obligation of formal resi-

[6] *Cf.* S. C. C., 1573—Richter, *Canones et Decreta Concilii Tridentini,* p. 38, n. 12.

[7] *Cf.* S. C. C., 1573—Richter, *Canones et Decreta Concilii Tridentini,* p. 38, n. 12.

[8] *Cf.* S. C. C., 17 December, 1881—*Thesaurus Resolutionum S. C. C.* Vol. CXL, p. 692.

[9] *De Parocho,* pars 1, c. VIII, n. 23.

[10] *Cf.* Garcia, *De Beneficiis Ecclesiasticis,* pars III, c. II, nn. 40-42; Henry, *De Residentia Beneficiatorum,* pp. 200, 201.

dence. It is evident that he may hold such a position during the two months' regular vacation given for a just cause but to employ him for a period extending over the two months does not seem to be in accord with the general norms of the law of residence. Hence the practice prevailing in some places of employing a pastor as chancellor, superintendent of schools, or superintendent of charities is not easily justified. According to all authors [11] the pastor must work on behalf of his flock and is bound to answer their calls when they ask for him personally. Those duties can, with difficulty, be carried out by one who is employed in any other position taking up most of his time and attention. When a pastor is appointed to a parish he is expected to be the spiritual guide and guardian of his parishioners.

### Article 5. Evident Utility to the Church or State

Under this heading will come such causes as the attendance at a General Council or Provincial Synod, the vindication of the pastor's rights or the obtaining of relief in an emergency. Sometimes it may be necessary for the pastor to be absent to attend as a delegate at Synods and Councils. Whenever such an absence extends beyond two months it seems the bishop may permit it. All the above mentioned causes are considered grave and are deemed sufficient excuses to justify absences extending over two months.

### Article 6. Absence Over Two Months

Whenever an absence of over two months takes place, besides having a grave cause, the pastor must have also the written permission of the Ordinary. He must also leave in his parish a suitable substitute approved by the Ordinary. It is well to state here that the written permission of the Ordinary is required for every absence extending over a week. Tacit permission is not sufficient.[12] In the case of a religious pastor the permission not only of the Ordinary, but also

[11] *Cf.* Schmalzgrueber, *Jus Canonicum Universum,* III, tit. 4, n. 4; Cocchi. *De Personis,* 419; Fanfani, *De Jure Parochorum,* 125; Smith, *Elements of Ecclesiastical Law,* 398; Bouix, *De Parocho,* 558; S. C. C., 10 March, 1742; Richter, *Canones et Decreta Concilii Tridentini,* p. 39, n. 20.

[12] *Cf.* Cappello, *De Administrativa Amotione Parochorum,* p. 51.

of the religious Superior must be obtained, and the substitute the pastor delegates to take care of the parish in his absence must be approved both by the Ordinary and the religious Superior. The pastor proposes the name of the substitute to the Ordinary. It is not sufficient if he merely states that a substitute has been provided to take his place. He must make known the identity of the substitute to the Ordinary.[13]

### Article 7. Power of the Substitute to Assist at Marriages

It is well to state here the power of the substitute to assist at marriages during the pastor's absence. The vicar substitute cannot validly assist at marriages until he has received the approval of the Ordinary. This was decided by the Commission for the Interpretation of the Code.[14] If he is a religious he may assist at marriages once he has received the approval of the Ordinary, even before he has received the approval of his Superior.[15] In case the pastor has to go away suddenly for a grave cause and is compelled to be absent for more than a week he is bound to inform the Ordinary as soon as possible of his absence, the cause for it and to make known to him the priest who is taking his place. In this case the *"sacerdos supplens"* may assist at marriages from the moment of his appointment by the pastor and may continue to do so until the Ordinary informs him to the contrary.[16]

### Article 8. Two Months' Absence

A cause is also required by the pastor, who is going to be absent for two months. Here, it seems, a grave cause is not required. The words of the Code indicate this *"nisi gravis causa, . . . diuturniorem absentiam requirat."* Hence, for the two months' ordinary vacation permitted annually any reasonable cause seems to suffice. According to authors [17] causes such as the calling on relatives, recuperation from illness, need of recreation and relaxation and the like will form

[13] *Cf.* Augustine, *Commentary* II, 548.

[14] 14 July, 1922—*A. A. S.*, XIV (1922), pp. 527, 528, ad II.

[15] *Ibid.*, ad III.

[16] *Ibid.*, ad IV.

[17] *Cf.* Bouix, *De Parocho*, p. 543; Smith, *Elements of Ecclesiastical Law*,

sufficient justification for a vacation of two months in ordinary circumstances. Circumstances may arise, where the Ordinary will be quite justified in refusing permission for a vacation of two months, *e. g.*, if it is difficult to provide for the necessities of the parish during the pastor's absence, or if there exists some difficulty, for the settling of which, the presence of the pastor, who is acquainted with the matter, is necessary. The Code leaves to the Ordinary the power to pass judgment as to whether the cause asserted by the pastor, who intends to be absent is sufficient. If the bishop refuses permission to a pastor, who thinks he has a just cause for absence, the pastor may have recourse to the Metropolitan, who will compel the bishop to grant the permission if a just cause exists.[18]

## Article 9. Absence for More than a Week

Here almost the same conditions hold as in longer absences. The pastor requires a cause, which of course need not be so serious as the causes required for longer absences. Here, too, as in the longer absences already dealth with, the pastor must leave a suitable substitute in the parish during his absence. The provision of the substitute conforms to the rules already stated and the pastor must conform to the same rules in obtaining the Ordinary's permission.

Canon 465, § 5, provides for cases in which the pastor is called away suddenly and is unable to apply for permission to be absent. If such an absence is to last for more than a week the pastor must inform the Ordinary by letter as to his absence and the cause for it. This paragraph indicates that, even if the pastor is called away suddenly and foresees that he will be absent for more than a week, he must provide a priest to take his place while he is away. It ordains that the pastor is to inform the Ordinary as to whom he left to attend to the needs of the parish in his absence. When the information with regard to the absence, the cause of it and the "*sacerdos supplens*" reaches the Ordinary he will make known to the pastor what is to be done in the case and the pastor is bound to abide by the decision of the Ordinary.

p. 398; Cocchi, pars II, *De Personis*, p. 397; Bouuaert, *Manuale Juris Canonici*, p. 318; Fanfani, *De Jure Parochorum*, p. 127.

[18] *Cf.* Boiux, *De Parocho*, 545.

### Article 10. Absence Less Than a Week

In case the pastor is absent for less than a week he must provide for the necessities of his parishioners during his absence. This can be done by asking the neighboring pastor to attend to sick calls and any other emergencies, that may arise.[19] Here the Code is silent on the question of obtaining permission of the Ordinary and the pastor is not bound to ask for leave of absence in such a case, unless diocesan statutes legislate to the contrary. If a Sunday or holyday intervened he would have to make provision to have Mass celebrated for the accommodation of his parishioners.[20]

### Article 11. Computation of Time of Absence

The time of absence of a pastor is to be calculated in integral days and the time of illegal absence is to be counted from the time the legitimate vacation ends.[21] If the two months' regular vacation are continuous, they are to be taken as they are in the calendar.[22] If the two months are taken intermittently they embrace a period of sixty days.[23] A day consists of twenty-four hours to be computed from midnight.[24] For example, if a pastor begins a continued vacation of two months on August 15th, the two months expire on the beginning of October 15th, although in all there are sixty-one days, because as was said above, two months, if continuous are to be taken as they are in the calendar. For the same reason, if the vacation begins on February 15th, the two months expire on April 15th, although the whole comprises fifty-nine days, except in the case of a Leap Year.

If a pastor is absent from six o'clock on Monday morning until six o'clock on Wednesday evening, he is absent only for one day, because a day consists of twenty-four continuous hours, to be calcu-

[19] *Cf.* Blat II, *De Personis*, p. 500.

[20] *Cf.* Fanfani, *De Jure Parochorum*, p. 129; Augustine, *Commentary* II, p. 548.

[21] *Cf.* Sartori, *Enchiridion Canonicum*, p. 53.

[22] Canon 34, § 3, n. 1.

[23] Canons 32, § 1; 34, § 2.

[24] Canon 32, § 1.

lated from midnight. The hours, which preceded the first midnight, namely, on Monday and the hours, which followed on midnight on Wednesday are not to be counted, according to Canon 32, § 1, nor are these hours to be added to future absences.[25]

After the regular vacation has expired, each absence of an entire day counts as illegal, unless it is in some way excused, because the time of illegal absence is to be computed in entire days after the regular vacation time, whether taken intermittently or continuously, ends.[26]

Hence a pastor loses his right to that part of his salary corresponding to the time of his illegal absence. Canon 2381, n. 1. Even if the absences, which are illegal, last only for a short time, or are not gravely culpable, the provision laid down in Canon 2381, n. 1, by which a pastor who is illegally absent incurs *ipso facto* loss of his salary in proportion to the time of his unlawful absence, seems to hold.[27]

To form a correct idea on this opinion one must first of all bear in mind that unlawful absence of pastors begins only after their legal vacation ends. Secondly, a pastor is permitted one or two days' absence each week and two or three hours' recreation every day. Thirdly, illegal absence is calculated in integral days only.[28] Hence, the loss of the pastor's income in proportion to the time of absence

[25] *Cf.* Fanfani, *De Jure Parochorum*, p. 128.

[26] S. C. C., 10 July, 1920, ad VI—*A. A. S.*, XII (1920), 365.

[27] S. C. C., 10 July, 1920, ad II—*A. A. S.*, XII (1920), 365. Since this decision was given in regard to the question of residence of canons it cannot be said to apply *in toto* to the residence of pastors. The obligation of a canon to residence is a matter that is definitely fixed by law. A canon is bound to attend the whole office in choir. If he fails to attend any part of it he is not fulfilling his obligation in regard to residence. On the other hand the pastor's obligation to residence is not so strictly defined. If he, *e.g.*, says Mass in the morning, attends to his catechetical instruction and the other duties that arise, he can hardly be said to violate the law of residence if he leaves his parish when he has fulfilled these duties. Hence the above decision of the Sacred Congregation of the Council does not apply so strictly to the pastor's obligation to residence as it does to the obligation of a canon to be present in choir at the whole office.

[28] *Cf.* S. C. C., 10 July, 1920, ad VI—*A. A. S.*, XII (1920), 365.

is incurred only when his absence takes place outside the above-mentioned concessions. Therefore, if he is absent for one or two days during the week or for a few hours every day he does not incur any loss of income. However, if he is absent, *e. g.*, for five or six days after his regular vacation ends, it seems he incurs the loss of his salary in proportion to that time, though the absence in itself might not be considered a grave violation of the law of residence. The pastor, who through illegal absence loses the right to his salary, is bound to hand it over to the Ordinary before a declaratory sentence. This is evident from the fact that the penalty is incurred *ipso facto*.[29]

In dealing with absence the question may be asked, may a pastor be excused altogether from his obligation to residence? It seems the Pope could dispense a pastor from his obligation but does not do so. The practice of the Roman Congregations according to Cocchi [30] is to grant an absence of six months while a serious impediment to residence exists. When this time has elapsed the pastor, while his absence may not be culpable, is compelled to resign. There is mention of a case [31] where a pastor was permitted an absence of five years, while the care of souls was provided for by the appointment of a vicar approved by the Ordinary. This vicar was obliged to reside in the parish from which the pastor was allowed leave of absence. The pastor, who was given the above dispensation was a man of outstanding merits, whose health was in danger of being impaired seriously by reason of the unsuitability of the climate. There was also danger that if he resigned from his parish it would be suppressed by the Government. The conclusion to be drawn is that the Holy See does not permit perpetual absence of a pastor. Temporary permission for absence may be obtained, but the cause for it must be based on very serious reasons.

[29] S. C. C., 10 July, 1920, ad VII—*A. A. S.*, XII (1920), 365.

[30] *De Personis*, pars I, p. 399.

[31] S. C. C., 26 April, 1879—*A. S. S.*, XII (1879), 364.

# CHAPTER X

## PROCEDURE AGAINST NON-RESIDENT PASTORS

### ARTICLE 1. PROCEDURE AGAINST PASTORS IN GENERAL

As was already seen, a pastor does not fulfill his obligation to residence, if he merely remains in his parish and leaves all the work to be carried out by his assistants. If the assistant vicar given to a pastor, who is incapable of discharging his duties properly, takes the place of the pastor in all the affairs of the parish, he has the same rights and duties as a pastor, with the exception of the application of the *Missa pro populo,* which obligation rests on the pastor himself.[1] The rights and duties of an assistant given to a pastor, who cannot take care of all the work of the parish on account of the great number of parishioners or for other reasons, depend upon diocesan statutes, the bishop's letter of appointment and the commission of the pastor. Unless the contrary is stated, the assistant must help the pastor in the general ministry of the parish with the exception of the *Missa pro populo.*[2]

Even when the pastor has assistants, his obligation to both formal and material residence does not cease. However, the procedure here is directed against non-observance of material residence. Hence, if the pastor remains in his parish and fails to carry out any of the duties of his office, though he may sin by such conduct, he does not come under the procedure mentioned here.[3] It is well to state here that there are two classes of pastors mentioned in Canon Law, one removable and the other irremovable, according to the stability with which they are established in their parishes. The fact that there is one class of pastors called *irremovable* does not mean that they cannot be deprived nor removed from their parishes. For the removal or deprivation of such, more formalities of law have to be observed than are employed in the removal or deprivation of removable pastors.

[1] *Cf.* Canon 475, §§ 1, 2.

[2] *Cf.* Canon 476, §§ 1-6.

[3] *Cf.* Coronata, *Institutiones Juris Canonici,* III, p. 532; Noval IV, *De Processibus,* p. 541; Suarez, *De Remotione Parochorum,* p. 133.

As a result of this distinction, a twofold mode of procedure presents itself here accordingly as the pastor is removable or irremovable.

**Canon 2168, § 1. Parochum, canonicum aliumve clericum, qui residentiae legem, qua ratione beneficii tenetur, negligat, Ordinarius moneat, et interim si agatur de parocho, eiusdem impensis provideat ne salus animarum detrimentum patiatur.**

**§ 2. In monitione Ordinarius recolat poenas quas incurrunt clerici non residentes itemque praescriptum can. 188, n. 8, et clerico significet ut intra congruum tempus ab eodem Ordinario definiendum residentiam instauret.**

*Ordinarius* here is understood in the sense of Canon 198. In this procedure, however, the vicar general cannot act without a special mandate of the bishop, since there is question here of the application of a penalty and the vicar general has not power to inflict penalties without a special mandate from the bishop.[4] This special mandate may be given to the vicar general, at least for the drawing up of the procedure, after the bishop himself has issued the monition to the non-resident pastor.[5] If the vicar general is given the mandate, he should not act independently of the bishop, as the Code [6] binds him to inform the bishop of his actions in regard to the discipline of both the clergy and laity.

It is well to give a few general ideas about the process to be employed here. First of all, it is not a judicial procedure, hence the formalities to be observed here are much simpler than the formalities employed in a trial. The persons to be present from the beginning are the Ordinary and notary. Afterwards, if necessary, as the case proceeds, the synodal examiners are to be called in. This will become clearer in the passages that follow.

In trials it is necessary for the *reus* to have an advocate.[7] In the

[4] *Cf.* Canon 2220, § 2.

[5] *Cf.* Wernz, *Jus Canonicum*, p. 742.

[6] Canon 365, § 1.

[7] *Cf.* Canon 1655, § 1.

present procedure, however, the intervention of advocates is ruled out. The pastor defends himself by his replies and allegation of excuses. He is not forbidden to consult privately advocates and others, whose advice would be of assistance to him in his defense.[8]

Before the bishop begins to proceed against a pastor, he must be certain that the pastor has violated the law of residence. This certainty can best be attained from the reports of the dean (*vicarius foraneus*), whose duty it is to see that the priests in his territory carry out their obligations in regard to the law of residence.[9] When the bishop attains this certainty, he issues an admonition to the offending pastor. Here the admonition is not a private paternal one, and hence is to be issued according to the norms of Canon 2143; that is, it is to be given either orally before the chancellor or some other official of the Curia, or before two witnesses, or by mail. A registered letter demanding a return receipt on its delivery will be the surest way of knowing that the pastor has been duly notified.[10] In the admonition the penalties, which non-resident clerics incur, are recalled. These penalties are laid down in Canon 2381, where it is stated that anyone, who obtains any office, benefice, or dignity, with the duty of residence attached to it, incurs *ipso facto*, for illegitimate absence, loss of all the fruits or revenue of the benefice or office in proportion to the time of the illegal absence. These fruits and income must be handed over to the Ordinary, who will devote them to some church or pious institution or to the poor. Furthermore, the non-resident shall be deprived of the office, benefice or dignity in accordance with the present Canons (2168-2175). In the admonition the Ordinary also reminds the pastor of the precept contained in Canon 188, n. 8, which states that an office becomes vacant by tacit resignation, if the cleric has unlawfully deserted the residence to which he is bound and, despite his Ordinary's warning has neither appeared, nor answered within a reasonable time fixed by the Ordinary, without having a legitimate cause for not appearing or not answering. The admonition also signifies that the pastor must resume residence within the time specified by the Ordinary.

[8] *Cf.* Suarez, *De Remotione Parochorum,* p. 136.

[9] *Cf.* Canon 447, § 1.

[10] *Cf.* Canon 1719; Suarez, *De Remotione Parochorum,* p. 140.

In the meantime the Ordinary must make provision, at the expense of the pastor, for the care of souls in the parish from which he is absent. Since the pastor by his lack of residence fails to provide for the care of souls, it is only right that the one who is appointed to assume the care of souls in his absence, should be paid at the expense of the pastor.[11]

The Ordinary is to provide for the care of souls immediately. He should not wait until he has received a reply to the admonition issued to the pastor. Detriment to souls may follow even when the absent pastor has assistants. The duty of the assistant is to aid the pastor and he lacks that authority, which is necessary for the proper fulfillment of the duties of the parish. Hence, Noval [12] says that even when the pastor has assistants the Ordinary should appoint a substitute, who will be responsible to him during the pastor's absence. One of the assistants in the parish can be appointed as the responsible substitute.

**Canon 2169. Si intra praestitutum terminum clericus nec residentiam instauret nec absentiae causas afferat, Ordinarius, servato praescripto can. 2149, declaret paroeciam aliudve beneficium vacare.**

After the admonition has been issued, various cases may arise, depending on whether the absent pastor resumes residence or gives excuses for his absence. It is only when he neither resumes residence nor gives reason for his absence that the Ordinary declares the parish vacant. Although the present canon specifies that the Ordinary shall declare the parish vacant, the prescription is laid down more for the sake of convenience and to avoid future difficulties than out of necessity, because by failure to obey the Ordinary's admonition or to give reasons for his absence, the pastor has already tacitly resigned his title to the parish and even if the Ordinary does not issue the declaration the parish becomes vacant *ipso facto*. Hence, in reality, it is not necessary for the Ordinary to declare the parish vacant.[13]

[11] *Cf.* Suarez, *De Remotione Parochorum*, p. 141.

[12] Noval IV, *De Processibus*, 546.

[13] *Cf.* Canon 188, n. 8.

The Ordinary should not proceed with the declaration to the effect that the parish is vacant unless he has first ascertained that the pastor has received the admonition and has not been prevented from replying.[14] If the admonition was issued by registered mail demanding a return receipt on its reception the Ordinary can be certain, when he receives the return receipt, that the pastor has been duly notified.[15] When the admonition is given orally the Ordinary will acquire his certainty from the acts drawn up by the notary.

Sometimes it may be difficult to ascertain whether the pastor received the admonition or not. To help in acquiring certainty in this matter, the Ordinary can seek the aid of the dean or of laymen of good standing, who will inquire as to whether the pastor refused to accept the admonition or hid at the time it was to be delivered.[16] If the pastor impedes the delivery of the admonition, either by hiding or by any other means, he is considered as duly notified.[17] If it happens that the pastor's whereabouts cannot be ascertained, it seems the only way in which he can be cited is by edict or public announcement. This is done by posting the citation at the doors of the Curia for a time to be determined by the prudent judgment of the Ordinary, and by inserting the summons in some public paper. If both cannot be done, either manner of citation suffices.[18] The Ordinary must also be certain that the pastor was not impeded in replying. This certainty can hardly be ascertained unless by questioning the pastor. This questioning could be carried out by men of good standing, or by the dean or some priest of the place where the pastor is at present.[19] If after all the inquiries, the Ordinary finds out that the pastor did not receive the admonition or was prevented from replying, he can settle the matter by either renewing the admonition or lengthening

[14] *Cf.* Canon 2149.

[15] *Cf.* Noval, IV, *De Processibus,* 498.

[16] *Cf.* Noval, IV, *De Processibus,* p. 499.

[17] *Cf.* Canon 2143, § 3; *A. A. S.,* XII (1920), 577; *Periodica,* X (1922), 256; *Jus Pontificium,* 1923, 125.

[18] *Cf.* Canon 1720; *A. A. S.,* XII (1920), 577.

[19] *Cf.* Coronata, *Institutiones Juris Canonici,* III, p. 511; Noval, IV, *De Processibus,* p. 499.

the time for an answer.[20] It sometimes may happen that the pastor will ask for some time to prepare his reasons for absence. The Code does not contemplate such a case here, but if the pastor makes such a request, the Ordinary can grant it, provided the pastor asks it before the time laid down by the Ordinary for returning has not already elapsed.[12]

When the time for returning has elapsed and the Ordinary has declared the parish vacant, the absent pastor has no longer any right to the parish and if he returns he is not to be admitted to it.[22] An unusual case could arise, if a pastor came back, even after a long time, and proved the existence of a just impediment, *e. g.*, if he were prevented by force or fear from returning to his parish. In such a case his title to his parish would not have perished and he should be allowed to return to it.[23] It is not likely that a case like this will arise if the preliminary instructions, regarding the admonition and the certainty that it was duly received and could be answered, are carried out properly.[24]

**Canon 2170. Si clericus residentiam instauret, Ordinarius, non modo debet, si absentia illegitima fuerit, ei infligere privationem fructuum pro tempore absentiae, de qua in can. 2381, sed potest etiam, si casus ferat, pro gravitate culpae eum congrue punire.**

This Canon considers the case where the pastor returns. If the pastor's absence has been unlawful the Ordinary must (*debet*) punish him by deprivation of his income in proportion to the time of absence. He may (*potest*) also if the case calls for it, inflict other penalties in proportion to the guilt of the pastor.

It is evident the Code contemplates here the case where the absence may be quite justified, *e. g.*, if the pastor was called away sud-

[20] *Cf.* Suarez, *De Remotione Parochorum,* p. 142; Coronata, *Institutiones Juris Canonici,* III, p. 535.

[21] *Cf.* Coronata, *Institutiones Juris Canonici,* III, p. 535.

[22] Wernz-Vidal, VI, *De Processibus,* p. 743.

[23] *Cf.* Suarez, *De Remotione Parochorum,* p. 142; Coronata, *Institutiones Juris Canonici,* III, p. 535.

[24] *Cf.* Canon 2149, § 1.

denly and had no opportunity of informing the Ordinary of his absence. It could also happen that absence for a longer time than that permitted by the Ordinary would become lawful, *e. g.*, if the pastor became ill during vacation, or was in some other way prevented from returning within the allotted time. Hence, the Ordinary should investigate as to whether the absence was lawful or not before he proceeds to declare the deprivation of the income.[25] If the absence is justified, no penalty may be inflicted. It is evident that if the absence was lawful the Ordinary imposes no penalties. If the absence was unlawful the Ordinary declares that the pastor has lost the right to his income during the time of absence. As far as the pastor is concerned this declaration is not necessary, because he is bound, even before a declaratory sentence, to turn the income over to the Ordinary.[26] The Ordinary in his declaration will determine the amount to be handed over to him in accordance with the time of illegal absence. Hence, if the income of the pastor is $1,000 per year, and the pastor has been illegally absent for six months the amount to be given up will be $500. According to Augustine [27] this seems to be too excessive, and he would allow the pastor to retain as much as was necessary for his support during the time of absence. This opinion, which seems to be based on charity, is hardly in consonance with the norms of the present canon binding, as it does, the Ordinary to inflict deprivation of the pastor's income in proportion to the time of absence as determined in Canon 2381, n. 1, which lays down that the pastor is to be deprived of *all* the fruits in proportion to the time of his illegal absence.

Besides declaring the *ipso facto* loss of the income, the Ordinary may inflict other congruous penalties. If the Ordinary decides to inflict these penalties he may employ such as are laid down in Canon 2298 or the remedies and penances contained in Canons 2306 and 2313.[28] Any further penalties that are inflicted should be in propor-

[25] *Cf.* Noval, IV, *De Processibus*, p. 548; Suarez, *De Remotione Parochorum*, p. 143.

[26] *Cf. A. A. S.*, XII, p. 365, ad VII.

[27] *Commentary* VII, p. 454.

[28] *Cf.* Rossi, *De Paroecia*, pp. 293, 294; Coronata, *Institutiones Juris Canonici*, III, p. 536.

tion to the guilt of the pastor. Hence, *per se, e. g.*, a pastor, who has been absent for a week or two or who has assistants in his parish, should not be punished as severely as one who has been absent for a month or two or who was the only priest in his parish.[29]

**Canon 2171. Si clericus residentiam non instauret, sed absentiae causas afferat, Ordinarius, accitis duobus examinatoribus et institutis, si opus fuerit, opportunis investigationibus, videre debet num causae sint legitimae.**

Here, if the pastor, instead of returning to the parish, gives reasons for his absence a new phase arises. The Ordinary calls in two of the synodal or pro-synodal examiners to discuss the excuses offered by the pastor, and to see if they are legitimate. The two examiners to be called in should be ones, who are neither inimical nor friendly to the pastor, in order that their opinion in the case may be based rather on justice than on sentiment.[30] Though the Ordinary is not bound to follow the opinion of the examiners here, it would seem that to act validly he has to call them in. This view is held by such authors as Coronata,[31] Noval,[32] Suarez [33] and Cocchi.[34] The opinion of these authors is based on Canon 5, n. 1, which lays down the following rule, when the law requires a Superior to seek the consent of some persons before acting.

If consent is required, any action taken by the Superior contrary to the vote of these persons is invalid. If consultation only is demanded (by words like *de consilio consultorum, audito capitulo, parocho,* etc.), it suffices for validity of the action, if the Superior consults the persons specified.

**Canon 105, n. 1. Si consensus exigatur, Superior contra earundem [personarum] votum invalide agit; si**

[29] *Cf.* Suarez, *De Remotione Parochorum,* p. 144.

[30] *Cf.* Noval IV, *De Processibus,* 493.

[31] *Institutiones Juris Canonici,* III, 536.

[32] IV, *De Processibus,* 493.

[33] *De Remotione Parochorum,* 145.

[34] III, *De Personis,* 43.

> **consilium tantum, per verba, ex. gr. *de consilio consultorum*, vel *audito Capitulo, parocho*, etc., satis est ad valide agendum ut Superior illas personas audiat.**

From this it seems to follow that if the hearing of the counsel is in itself sufficient, then, *vi sensus contrarii* its omission becomes insufficient for the desired validity of the act. In the canon to be dealt with here (2171) the words used are *accitis duobus examinatoribus*, which seem to imply the same thing as *audito* in Canon 105, n. 1.

There are, however, other authors, who hold for the less strict view in regard to Canon 105, n. 1.[35] Their view gives a basis for doubting as to whether it is necessary for validity to call in the examiners in Canon 2171. Hence, if the Ordinary does not summon them it cannot be said with certainty that his action is invalid.

The Ordinary discusses the alleged reasons with the two examiners, and if necessary, makes further investigation concerning the absence of the pastor. Sometimes it may happen that the pastor will assert, on the testimony of doctors, that he was prevented by illness from returning to his parish. If the Ordinary becomes suspicious of such medical testimony, he may consult other doctors to ascertain the truth in the matter. Since the investigation is not necessary for the procedure there is no obligation on the part of the Ordinary to carry it out. His prudence and sense of justice will dictate what he is to do according to the circumstances of each particular case.[36]

The Code does not say that the examiners are to be consulted on the results of the investigation, if it is made, hence the Ordinary is free to judge by himself in regard to the information following on it. If the pastor presents two or three witnesses to further strengthen the reasons he alleges for his absence, the Ordinary may hear them, unless after consulting the examiners, he thinks they are presented to delay the case. Since the proceeding is summary, the Ordinary should be slow to give it the semblance of a solemn trial, by admit-

[35] *Cf.* Vermeersch-Creusen, *Epitome Juris Canonici,* III, p. 173; Bastnagel, *The Appointment of Parochial Adjutants and Assistants,* p. 228; Boudinhon, *Jus Pont.* VIII (1928), 29-35; Wernz-Vidal, *Jus Canonicum,* II, *De Personis,* p. 35.

[36] *Cf.* Wernz-Vidal, VI, *De Processibus,* p. 744, footnote.

ting many witnesses. If witnesses are admitted they should be sworn.[37]

**Canon 2172. Si, auditis examinatoribus, Ordinarius censeat adductas causas non esse legitimas, rursus clerico praefigat terminum intra quem redire debet, salva semper privatione fructuum pro tempore absentiae.**

In determining the time within which the pastor is to return the Ordinary should indicate to the pastor, the reasons why his excuses were rejected. This seems right in view of the fact that the irremovable pastor has a further chance to defend himself by the allegation of new excuses.[38] When there is question of a removable pastor, who has been unlawfully absent, the Ordinary is to deprive him of his salary in proportion to the time of absence. This time of absence is to be computed, not from the moment at which the reasons were rejected as illegitimate, but from the time at which the pastor's illegal absence began, because since the excuses alleged by the pastor were considered illegitimate, his absence was illegal, not from the moment at which the causes were rejected, but during the whole time of absence for which they were alleged. Hence he becomes subject to the *ipso facto* loss of his income as laid down in Canon 2381, § 1.[39]

If, on the contrary, the Ordinary finds that the reasons were legitimate no penalty is to be inflicted on the pastor, because with a sufficiently excusing cause, absence becomes lawful.[40] A case could arise, where a pastor, though guilty of illegal absence, would so successfully defend himself, that the Ordinary could not see his way to inflict any penalty or oblige him to restitution of his income. Even in such a case the pastor is still bound to restitution, though he would not according to Coronata [41] be bound to manifest his guilt to the Ordinary.

[37] *Cf.* Canon 2145.

[38] *Cf.* Noval, IV, *De Processibus*, p. 550.

[39] *Cf.* Noval, IV, *De Processibus*, p. 550.

[40] *Cf.* Wernz-Vidal, VI, *De Processibus*, p. 744; Coronata III, p. 537.

[41] *Institutiones Juris Canonici*, III, p. 537; *cf.* Muniz, I, *Procedimentios Ecclesiasticos*, p. 624.

**Canon 2173. Si parochus amovibilis intra praescriptum tempus non redierit, Ordinarius statim procedere potest ad paroeciae privationem; si redierit, Ordinarius det ei praeceptum ne rursus discedat sine scripta sua licentia sub poena privationis paroeciae ipso facto incurrenda.**

Before proceeding to deprive the pastor of his parish, the Ordinary should be certain that the pastor has received the admonition telling him to return within a specified time, and that he is not impeded in any way from responding to the request to resume residence.[42] From the word *potest* it can be taken for granted that the Ordinary is still free to consider new reasons, if the pastor should present them, but he is not bound to do so and he may immediately, without more ado, deprive the removable pastor of his parish. Charity or equity might impel him to give further consideration to new reasons if they are alleged and to allow some delay to the pastor if, he asks for time to prepare new excuses or explanations for his absence.[43]

If the pastor returns, the Ordinary gives him a precept not to leave the parish again without written permission, under penalty of *ipso facto* deprivation of the parish. Since this precept is an act of the process, it should ordinarily be given before the notary, who will consign it to the acts of the case.[44] If, however, the pastor, who has resumed residence, lives a long distance from the Curia or if for any other reason the precept cannot be given to him before the notary, it may be sent to him by registered mail demanding a signed receipt to the effect that it was received.[45] The notary should take a general note of the contents of the precept and when the signed receipt comes back he should consign it, together with the notes on the tenor of the

[42] *Cf.* Canon 2149; Coronata, *Institutiones Juris Canonici,* III, p. 537; Rossi, *De Paroecia,* pp. 295, 296.

[43] *Cf.* Noval, IV, *De Processibus,* p. 551; Suarez, *De Remotione Parochorum,* p. 147.

[44] *Cf.* Canon 2142; Augustine, VIII, *Commentary,* p. 455; Suarez, *De Remotione Parochorum,* p. 147.

[45] *Cf.* Canon 1719.

precept, to the acts of the case.[46] From this canon it would seem that the precept should impose a life-long threat. Since, however, it is a difficult precept to observe, it should be imposed only for such time as it will take the pastor to make amends for his past negligence. Coronata [47] maintains that it should not be imposed for longer than one or two years. His opinion seems to be the correct one to follow, as the multiplication and prolongation of precepts of the kind above mentioned tend to instil a disregard rather than a docile observance of the law.[48] As long as the precept lasts it binds the pastor to obtain the written permission of the Ordinary, whenever he wishes to be absent from his parish. Hence, he will be bound to apply for permission, when otherwise he could leave without the Ordinary's consent, *e. g.*, if he were to be absent for five or six days.

Since penalties are inflicted only for crimes, if the pastor by disregard of this precept does not commit a canonical offense, *i. e.*, an external and morally imputable violation of a law, to which at least an indeterminate canonical sanction is attached,[49] he escapes the penalty of deprivation.

Precepts of an ecclesiastical superior imposed on his subject with the threat of penalty in case of disobedience have the effect that the transgression ordinarily becomes an offense.[50] If through grave fear, necessity, or grave inconvenience, the pastor is compelled to be absent, without the written permission of the Ordinary, the penalty does not bind him, because grave fear and the other causes mentioned above excuse as a rule from liability, when there is question of an ecclesiastical law. Therefore the pastor is not bound by the precept when he is satisfied that one of these excusing causes is present. If, however, the Ordinary determines that the pastor erred in his judgment as to the gravity of the excuse, the pastor will have to sub-

[46] *Cf.* Noval, IV, *De Processibus*, p. 552; Coronata, *Institutiones Juris Canonica*, III, p. 537.

[47] *Institutiones Juris Canonici*, III, p. 537.

[48] *Cf.* Augustine, VIII, *Commentary*, p. 455; Muniz, I, *Procedimentios Ecclesiasticos*, p. 148; Suarez, *De Remotione Parochorum*, p. 148; Cocchi, *De Processibus*, p. 625.

[49] Canon 2195.

[50] Woywod, *Commentary*, II, 401.

mit to the deprivation of the parish, as crass ignorance, error, or lack of due diligence does not excuse from penalties *latae sententiae.*[51] In taking recourse against the deprivation the pastor could mention why he was deprived of the parish in this case. In case of emergency, when it is impossible for the pastor to ask for permission to be absent the precept does not urge, as no one is bound to the impossible. To provide for circumstances when it will be difficult for the pastor to seek the permission of the Ordinary to be absent, it would be well, if the Ordinary would endow the dean or the pastor living nearest the one on whom the precept is placed, with power to grant permission in such cases, with the obligation of notifying the Ordinary as soon as possible.[52] According to Coronata [53] the penalty of deprivation of the parish does not extend to short absences of one or two days a week, provided they do not occur frequently. That opinion seems to lessen very much the binding force of the precept, which is imposed to correct the pastor's abuse of the law of residence.[54] If the Ordinary has committed to the dean or nearest pastor power to grant permission, when the occasion arises, the pastor subject to the precept will have ample opportunity to obtain leave, when circumstances call for absence of a day or two.

## Article 2. Procedure Against Irremovable Pastor

Since an irremovable pastor is given by law a further chance to defend himself, if he has been absent, a new phase in the present procedure arises.

> **Canon 2174, § 1. Si clericus, qui beneficium inamovibile obtinet, residentiam non instauret, sed novas alleget deductiones, Ordinarius eas cum eisdem examinatoribus ad examen revocet ad normam can. 2171.**

[51] *Cf.* Canons 2229, § 3, nn. 1, 2; 2202, § 3; Noval, IV, *De Processibus,* 552.

[52] *Cf.* Wernz-Vidal, VI, *De Processibus,* 745.

[53] *Institutiones Juris Canonici,* III, p. 537.

[54] *Cf.* De Meester, *Juris Canonici,* p. 290.

**§ 2. Si nec ipsae legitimae habitae fuerint, posthabitis quibusvis aliis deductionibus, Ordinarius clerico praecipiat ut intra tempus praescriptum vel iterum praescribendum redeat sub poena privationis beneficii ipso facto incurrenda.**

**§ 3. Si non redeat, Ordinarius eum beneficium privatum declaret; si redeat, Ordinarius idem det praeceptum de quo in can. 2173.**

If the irremovable pastor presents new excuses, which prevented him from obtaining written permission to be absent or from returning on being notified to do so, the Ordinary discusses these reasons with the two examiners as already mentioned in Canon 2171. New reasons for absence could arise from such circumstances as illness, which has become graver since the pastor's first excuses were rejected, serious illness of the pastor's parents and the like. It is useless for the pastor to assert the same reasons as have already been rejected as illegitimate.[55] If, after the Ordinary and the two examiners have investigated the new excuses alleged by the pastor, they are found to be insufficient, the Ordinary, without further proceedings, issues a precept to the pastor to resume residence within the time fixed in the first admonition or within a time now to be prescribed, under penalty of the deprivation of the parish to be incurred *ipso facto*. Here the Ordinary is not left free to institute further investigation, because the pastor, having received notice of the rejection of his former excuses, can no longer be ignorant of his obligation to resume residence. Hence, no further questioning regarding his absence is necessary.[56] Here the command to return is given in the same way as already stated in the commentary dealing with the admonition mentioned in Canon 2168, § 2. An authentic record of its administration and its tenor should be preserved among the acts of the case.[57] Non-observance of the precept carries with it *ipso facto* deprivation of the parish.[58] If the pastor obeys the precept

[55] *Cf.* Noval, o. c., p. 553; Coronata, o. c., p. 538; Suarez, o. c., p. 149.

[56] *Cf.* Noval, o. c., p. 553.

[57] *Cf.* Canon 2143, § 2.

[58] *Cf.* Suarez, *De Remotione Parochorum*, p. 149.

and resumes residence the Ordinary is to deprive him of his salary in proportion to the time of absence.[59] He may also punish him by the infliction of other congruous penalties according to the gravity of his fault.[60] The Ordinary also gives the pastor a precept not to leave the parish again without his written permission under penalty of losing the parish *ipso facto.* This precept follows the same rules and is subject to the same interpretation as that given for the precept issued to the removable pastor according to the norms of Canon 2173.

If, on the contrary, the pastor does not resume residence, the Ordinary declares him deprived of his parish. The general prescription of Canon 2223, § 4. (1) which says that it is as a rule left to the discretion of the Superior to declare a penalty *latae sententiae* does not hold here, because the same Canon 2223, § 4. (2) makes a further provision, namely, that if the public good demands it, the Superior must declare the penalty.

(1) *Poenam latae sententiae declarare generatim committitur prudentiae Superioris.*

(2) *Bono communi ita exigente, sententia declaratoria dari debet.*

The pastor who does not return to his parish after he has been duly notified and all the other requirements of law have been carried out, loses his title to his parish and the common good demands that a pastor, who has not a title should not be allowed to remain in his parish.[61]

**Canon 2175. Neutro in casu Ordinarius beneficium vacare declaret, nisi postquam, perpensis una cum examinatoribus discessus rationibus quas clericus forte allegaverit, eiusdem Ordinarii licentiam in scriptis ab eodem clerico peti potuisse constiterit.**

The Ordinary shall not proceed to declare the parish of either a removable or irremovable pastor vacant, until he has discussed with the examiners the reasons the pastor may have alleged for being

[59] *Cf.* Commentary on Canon 2172.

[60] *Cf.* Commentary on Canon 2170.

[61] *Cf.* Noval, o. c., p. 554.

absent, and until he has established the fact that the pastor could have obtained permission before going away. Rare cases might arise, where a pastor might be deprived of his parish, though he was guilty of no fault in the case, *e. g.*, if through force or fear he was compelled to leave his parish and by the same means was prevented from communicating with the Ordinary, or if, as is provided for in Canon 465, § 5, he was called away suddenly and then, through the cutting off of postal facilities, his communication notifying the Ordinary, and giving the reasons for his absence, became lost or delayed for a long time.[62] Hence arises the necessity of the discussion provided for in the present canon. If the discussion with the examiners reveals that the pastor was prevented from notifying the Ordinary of his absence, then the pastor has not incurred any guilt because his absence in the case was not blameworthy, and hence there is no foundation for proceeding against him.[63] The consultation of the examiners seems to be necessary for validity as already stated.[64] They are to discuss not only any reasons that the pastor may have given for his absence, but even if he gave no reasons, they should investigate, if necessary, as to his guilt.[65] Suarez [66] says that in the strict sense of the law the examiners are to be consulted only when the pastor alleges reasons for being absent.

However, since the deprivation of a parish is a serious matter, which should not be carried out until everything possible has been done to certify that the pastor is really guilty of grave fault by his absence, it seems that the Ordinary should always investigate with the aid of the examiners, as to whether the pastor is guilty or not, even when the pastor brought forward no excuses. The same examiners should be called in here as already participated in the discussion, because they should be the better able to judge from their previous knowledge of the merits or demerits of the case.[67] When the

[62] *Cf.* Coronata, o. c., p. 539.

[63] *Cf.* Noval, *De Processibus,* 554; Coronata, *Institutiones Juris Canonici,* III, 539; Rossi *De Paroecia,* 296; Augustine VII, *Commentary,* 456; Muniz, III, *Procedimientos Eclesiasticos,* 623; Suarez, *De Remotione Parochorum,* 150.

[64] *Cf.* Commentary on Canon 2171.

[65] *Cf.* Coronata, *Institutiones Juris Canonici,* III, 539.

[66] *De Remotione Parochorum,* 151.

[67] Suarez, *De Remotione Parochorum,* 150.

pastor's guilt in leaving without the permission of the Ordinary and in not returning when notified to do so is established with certainty, then the Ordinary deprives him of his parish.

### Article 3. Recourse Against the Decree of Deprivation

Against the decree of deprivation by the Ordinary, the pastor may have recourse to the Holy See, according to the norms of Canon 2146,[68] about which it is well to make a few remarks here. This canon in speaking of the decree of the Ordinary in the removal and transfer of pastors and in proceedings against clerics for non-observance of the law of residence, against clerics, who are guilty of concubinage and against pastors negligent in their pastoral duties, determines that from the final decree in these cases there is but one remedy in law, namely, recourse to the Holy See. In case of recourse all the acts of the process are to be forwarded to the Holy See and pending the recourse to be made within ten days the Ordinary cannot validly give permanently to another the parish or benefice of which the cleric was deprived. Here there is mention of a decree, not a sentence. Against a sentence the remedy is generally appeal to a higher tribunal, but against a final decree of the Ordinary one cannot appeal to a higher tribunal but must have recourse to the Holy See. Hence the Tribunal of the Rota has nothing to do with the recourse of a pastor against the decree of deprivation issued aganist him for non-observance of residence. The proper authority to deal with the recourse is the Sacred Congregation to which it belongs.[69]

The Congregation to which the appeal is sent varies according to the following cases: (a) The Sacred Congregation of the Council

[68] Canon 2146, § 1. A definitivo decreto unicum datur juris remedium, idest recursus ad Sedem Apostolicam.

§ 2. Quo in casu ad Sanctam Sedem omnia acta processus transmittenda sunt.

§ 3. Pendente recursu, Ordinarius paroeciam vel beneficium quo clericus privatus sit, alii stabiliter conferre valide nequit.

[69] *Cf.* Canon 1601.

is competent to receive the recourse of secular pastors; (b) The Sacred Congregation of Religious is the competent congregation to deal with the recourse of pastors, who belong to a religious order or congregation; (c) It is the Sacred Congregation for the Propagation of the Faith that is competent to deal with recourse of pastors, who are subject to that congregation.[70]

The recourse of a pastor against the decree of deprivation of his parish for non-observance of residence is *in devolutivo, i. e.*, the deprivation with all its effects, save one, remains binding. The one effect, which is *in suspensivo* in the decree of deprivation, is that the Ordinary cannot validly confer the parish permanently on another when the pastor, who has been deprived of it fulfills certain conditions.

The conditions the pastor must fulfill, in order that the Ordinary may not be able to validly confer the parish on another, are (a) he must have recourse within ten days; (b) he must notify the Ordinary that he is interposing recourse against the decree of deprivation. If the pastor does not fulfill these two conditions the parish may be conferred permanently on another. The Sacred Congregation of the Council was asked within what time a pastor must have recourse in order to benefit from the provision of Canon 2146, § 3.

The Sacred Congregation replied that the recourse must be taken within ten days (*tempus utile*) from the time the notification of deprivation or removal from the parish was made known to the pastor. The ten days are to be calculated as in Canon 34, § 3, n. 3, and Canon 35. The Ordinary should be informed by the pastor that he is interposing recourse.[71] Though the limitation of a prescribed time for having recourse, as distinguished from appeal, is unusual in Canon Law, it has in this case a special reason. Grave inconveniences could follow if a pastor, who is deprived of his parish, signified his intention of having recourse and then waited for a long time before having the recourse.[72] The ends of justice would be frustrated by such action and the power of the Ordinary would be im-

[70] *Cf.* Suarez, *De Remotione Parochorum*, pp. 17, 18.

[71] S. C. C., 14 January, 1924—*A. A. S.*, XVI (1924), 165.

[72] *Cf.* Suarez, *De Remotione Parochorum*, 18.

peded and it is not the wish of the Church that justice be interfered with by dilatory measures of this kind. Therefore it is but just that a definite limit should be set to the time allowed the pastor if he wishes to avail of the provision of Canon 2146, § 3.

*Tempus utile* means that time for the exercise or prosecution of one's rights does not lapse, if one is ignorant of his rights or could not act at the time. Hence if the pastor was unaware of the fact that he should have recourse within ten days in order to benefit from the provision of Canon 2146, § 3, or if he was unable through sickness or any other excuse to avail himself of the concession, the ten days (*tempus utile*) do not begin to count until he is aware of or able to avail himself of his right.[73] It seems that the pastor is not to be presumed ignorant of his rights here and if he claims ignorance the obligation of proving it rests on him.

*Tempus utile* can be interrupted. If the pastor becomes seriously ill, *e. g.*, five days after he became aware of his rights, so that he is prevented for three weeks from having recourse, the *tempus utile* will begin to count again only when he is sufficiently recovered to make use of his rights, and he still has five days within which he can have recourse.

The day on which the pastor receives the notification of deprivation does not count in the computation of the ten days, so that the pastor has ten complete days to interpose recourse after he receives the decree of deprivation. Hence, *e. g.*, if the decree is received on March 15th, he would be allowed to have recourse any time before midnight on March 25th. If the pastor does not fulfill the above conditions, namely, have recourse within ten days (*tempus utile*) and notify the Ordinary of his having recourse, the Ordinary may validly confer the parish permanently on another.[74] Therefore if the pastor interposes recourse after the *tempus utile* has elapsed, the recourse is *in devolutivo* in *all its effects*.

Except in so far as paragraph 3 of Canon 2346 is concerned, the time limit, within which one must have recourse, is not determined. In general a recourse may be made at any time and is not subject

[73] *Cf.* Woywod, *Commentary* I, p. 21; Noval, *De Processibus*, 449.

[74] Suarez, *De Remotione Parochorum*, 20.

to the *fatalia legis*. By the *fatalia legis* is meant fixed periods of time upon the lapse of which the law denies the right to sue.[75] Since all are free to approach the Holy See at any time,[76] it follows that the Holy See is not bound by the *fatalia legis*. Therefore the Holy See will receive a recourse at any time. Hence the pastor, who has been deprived of his parish for the non-observance of residence, may have recourse against the decree of deprivation at any time, except when he wishes to avail himself of the provision of Canon 2146, § 3. If he wishes to avail himself of this privilege his recourse must take place within ten days (*tempus utile*). When he fails to avail himself of this privilege afforded by having recourse within ten days all the effects of the decree of deprivation remain and the recourse in all its effects is *in devolutivo*.

### Article 4. Transmission of the Acts

When the Ordinary receives notice of the legitimate recourse, he is bound to send the acts of the procedure to the Holy See, namely to the competent congregation in the case. If the acts are not sent spontaneously by the Ordinary, the Holy See will ask for them when it receives the recourse. In Canon 1642, § 1, a distinction is made between the *acta causae*, which refer to the merits of the case, *e. g.*, decisions and all the proofs and the *acta processus*, which relate to the form of the procedure, *e. g.*, the summons, declaration and notices. Since Canon 2146, § 2, determines that all the acts of the procedure are to be sent to the Holy See, the question arises here as to what is meant by *omnia acta processus*. Here *omnia acta processus* means that all the acts both of the case and of the procedure are to be sent.[77] They will include, then, the proofs of non-residence, the admonitions, the pastors excuses, the precepts and the decree of deprivation. If all the acts are not sent the Holy See would be unable to know with certainty that all the prescriptions of the

[75] *Cf.* Canon 1634.

[76] *Cf.* Canon 1569.

[77] *Cf.* Suarez, *De Remotione Parochorum*, 22; Noval, IV, *De Processibus*, 456; Coronata, *Institutiones Juris Canonici*, III, 499.

canons dealing with the process against the non-resident pastor were carried out as demanded.

If the Holy See after examining the recourse reverses the decree of deprivation issued against the pastor, various hypotheses may arise. If the pastor had recourse within ten days his parish will still remain vacant and he can return to it without any necessity for a new provision. On the other hand, if the pastor has recourse after ten days and the decree of the Ordinary is not upheld, the pastor will require a new installation if he returns to the same parish, because after the ten days have passed the pastor has lost his right to his parish.[78] If, in the meantime, the parish has been conferred permanently on another, the Holy See will make provision as to what is to be done in the case, probably by commanding the Ordinary to give the pastor a new parish of equal standing or merit.

If the Holy See declares that the deprivation was invalid, the pastor has never lost his right to his parish and it could not be validly conferred on another in such a case. According to Suarez,[79] if the Ordinary knows that a pastor has taken recourse, even after ten days have elapsed, he should not confer the parish on another, out of respect to the Holy See. It seems he should wait to see what the outcome of the recourse will be. This seems to be a logical mode of action, as it may save many difficulties later on, especially if the decree of deprivation is declared invalid or is not upheld by the Holy See. There is, however, no obligation on the Ordinary to follow this mode of acting and if he feels that by waiting for the outcome of the decision by the Holy See, serious consequences may arise in the vacant parish, he may confer it on another immediately.[80]

[78] *Cf.* Noval, *De Processibus*, p. 457.

[79] *Cf.* Canon 150, § 1, Suarez, *De Remotione Parochorum*, p. 23.

[80] *Cf.* Canon 204.

# BIBLIOGRAPHY


## Sources

*Acta Apostolicae Sedis* (A. A. S.), Romae, 1909.

*Acta et Decreta Concilii Provincialis Portlandensis in Oregon Quarti*, 1932.

*Actae Sanctae Sedis* (A. A. S.), 41 vols., Romae, 1865-1908.

*Bullarium SSmi Domini Nostri Benedicti Papae XIV*, 4 vols., 4 ed., Venetiis, 1778.

*Canones et Decreta Concilii Tridentini*, 19 ed., Taurini, 1913.

*Codex Juris Canonici Pii X Pontificis Maximi iussu digestu. Benedict Papae XV auctoritate promulgatus*, Romae, 1918.

*Codex Juris Canonici Fontes*, 6 vols., Romae, 1923-1932.

*Corpus Juris Canonici, Editio Lipsiensis II*, 2 vols., Lipsiae, 1922.

*Corpus Juris Civilis*, 3 vols., Berolini, 1928-1929.

*Liber Sextus Decretalium, una cum Clementinis et Extravagantibus earumque glossis restitutis*, Romae, 1582.

Mansi, Joannes Dominicus, *Sacrorum Conciliorum Nova et Amplissima Collectio*, 53 vols., Parisiis, 1901-1927.

Migne, Jacques Paul, *Patrologia Latina* (MPL), 221 vols., Parisiis, 1858-1864.

Pallottini, Salvator, *Collectio Omnium Conclusionum et Resolutionum, S. C. C.*, 17 vols., Romae, 1868-1893.

Richter, Aemilius, *Canones et Decreta Concilii Tridentini*, Lipsiae, 1853.

*Thesaurus Resolutionum Sacrae Congregationis Concilii*, 167 vols., Romae, 1718-1908.

## References

Alphonsus, Saint, *Theologia Moralis*, 10 vols., Mechlinae, 1852.

(Bachofen) Charles Augustine, *A Commentary on the New Code of Canon Law*, 8 vols., St. Louis, 1918-1922.

Barbosa, Ubaldus, *De Parocho*, Romae, 1824.

Bargilliat, M, *Praelectiones Juris Canonici*, 37 ed., 2 vols., Parisiis, 1923.

Bastnagel, Clement, *The Appointment of Parochial Adjutants and Assistants*, Washington, D. C., 1930.

Benedict XIV, *De Synodo Dioecesana*, 2 vols., Romae, 1806.

Bingham, Joseph, *Origines Ecclesiasticae*, Londonii, 1711.

Blat, Albertus, *Commentarium Textus Juris Canonici*, 6 vols., Romae, 1921-1927.

Bouix, D., *Tractatus de Parocho*, Parisiis, 1855.

Bouuaert, F.-Simenon, G., *Manuale Juris Canonici*, 3 ed., 3 vols., Leodii, 1931.

Cappello, Felix M., *De Administrativa Amotione Parochorum*, Romae, 1911.

Chelodi, Joannes, *Jus de Personis*, 2 ed., Tridenti, 1927.

Cocchi, Guidus, *Commentarium in Codicem Juris Canonici ad usum scholarum*, 8 vols., Augustae Taurinorum, 1925-1927.

Cornelius a Lapide, *Commentarium in Sacram Scripturam*, vol. XIX, Mediolani, 1870.

Coronata, M., *Institutiones Juris Canonici*, Turin, 1923.

Devoti, Joannes, *Institutionum Canonicarum*, Libri IV, Leodii, 1860.

DeMeester, A., *Juris Canonici et Juris Canonici-Civilis Compendium*, 3 vols., Bruges, 1921-1928.

Deshayes, F., *Memento Juris Ecclesiastici*, Parisiis, 1902.

Fagnanus, Prosperus, *Commentarium in V Libros Decretalium*, 4 vols., Venetiis, 1696.

Fanfani, L., *De Jure Parochorum*, Taurini, Romae, 1924.

Ferraris, F. L., *Bibliotheca Prompta*, 8 vols., Parisiis, 1858.

Garcias, Nicolas, *De Beneficiis Ecclesiasticis*, 2 vols., Venetiis, 1618.

Giraldus, U., *Expositio Juris Pontificii*, Romae, 1769.

Henry, Ludovicus, *De Residentia Beneficiatorum*, Luvanii, 1862.

Koudelka, C. J., *Pastors, Their Rights and Duties*, Washington, D. C., 1921.

Makee, Ch., *Institutiones Juris Canonici*, 2 vols., Romae, 1897.

Maroto, Phillipus, *Institutiones Juris Canonici ad Normam Novi Codicis*, 2 vols., Romae, 1919-1921.

Muniz, T., *Procedimientos Ecclesiasticos*, 3 vols., Sevillae, 1930.

Noval, Josephus, *Commentarium Juris Canonici, Liber IV, De Processibus*, Romae, 1920.

Oesterle, Gerardus, *Praelectiones Juris Canonici*, Romae, 1931.

Pirhing, Henricus, *Jus Canonicum*, 5 vols., Dillingae, 1722.

Pistocchi, Marius, *De Re Beneficiali*, Taurini, 1928.

Reiffenstuel, Anacletus, *Jus Canonicum Universum*, 4 vols., Venetiis, 1735.

Rossi, J., *De Paroecia*, Romae, 1923.

Sartori, Cosmas, *Enchiridion Canonicum*, Hankow, 1926.

Schmalzgrueber, F., *Jus Ecclesiasticum Universum*, 12 vols., Romae, 1825.

Sipos, Stephanus, *Enchiridion Juris Canonici*, Pecs, 1926.

Smith, S. B., *Elements of Ecclesiastical Law*, 4 ed., 3 vols., New York, 1881.

Suarez, P. Emmanuele, O.P., *De Remotione Parochorum*, Romae, 1931.

Thomassin, L., *Vetus et Nova Ecclesiae Disciplina*, 10 vols., Magonatiaci, 1787.

Vecchiotti, Sept. M., *Institutiones Canonicae*, 18 ed., Taurini-Romae, 1886.

Vermeersch-Creusen, *Epitome Juris Canonici*, 4 ed., 3 vols., Mechliniae-Romae, 1929.

Wernz, Franciscus, *Jus Decretalium*, 6 vols., Romae, 1906-1913.

Wernz, F.-Vidal, P., *Jus Canonicum*, Romae, 1927-1928.

Woywod, Stanislaus, O.F.M., *A Practical Commentary on the New Code of Canon Law*, 2 vols., New York, 1926.


## Periodicals


*Ius Pontificium*, Romae, 1921.

*Periodica de Re Morali, Canonica Liturgica*, Romae et Brugis, 1912.

UNIVERSITAS CATHOLICA AMERICAE

WASHINGTON, D. C.

FACULTAS JURIS CANONICI

No. 97

1935

## ALPHABETICAL INDEX


Absence in general, 39.
  over two months, 42.
  two months, 43.
  a week or more, 44.
  less than a week, 45.
Acts of case, 67.
  transmission of, 67.
Admonition, 50.
  impeding of, 52.
Alexander III, his legislation on residence, 9.
Bishop, his permission necessary for absence, 12.
  written permission of, 42.
  his refusal to give permission, 44.
Causes for absence, before Code, 11, 13.
  after Code, 39-42.
Certainty, required before Ordinary proceeds against pastor, 50, 58.
Chancellor, should not be pastor, 41.
Charity, as cause for absence, 11, 40.
Citation for non-observance of residence, 17, 18.
*Concursus* for pastor's office, 13.
Council of Trent and residence, 14-19.
  in regard to obligation, 14, 15, 16.
  in regard to punishment, 18, 19.
Danger, as cause for absence, 12.
  if common does not excuse, 40.
Deprivation for non-residence, 17.
Dispensation from residence, 47.
Epidemic, as cause for absence, 41.
Examiners, consultation of, 55, 56, 63.
*Fatalia legis*, 67.
Formal residence, 4, 35, 36.
Ill-health, as cause for absence, 40, 41.
Innocent III, his legislation on residence, 9, 10.
Law by which pastors are bound to residence, 22-27.
Material residence, 4, 5.
Notary, should be present for procedure, 49.
Obedience, as cause for absence, 11, 41, 42.
Obligation to residence is grave, 32.
*Ordinarius*, proper one for procedure, 49.
Papal constitutions,
  *In Suprema*, 20.
  *Cupientes*, 20.
  *Ad Militantes*, 20, 21.
  *Firmandis*, 21.
Parish,
  development of, 6.
  loss of, 51.
  residence outside of, 37.
Parish house, residence in, 33, 34.
  residence outside of, 36, 37.
Pastors,
  development of, 6.
  division of, 48.
Poverty, as cause for absence, 41.
Precept in procedure, 58, 61.
  duration of, 59, 60.
Procedure in general against non-residents, 48-64.
  against irremovable pastor, 60, 64.
Recourse against deprivation of parish, 64, 65, 66.
  proper Congregation to receive, 64, 65.
  *in devolutivo*, 65.
Reasons for absence, assertion of, 55.
  if legitimate, 57.
Recreation, absence for, 34, 35.

Residence,
notion of, 3.
division of, 4.
development of, 6, 7, 8,
obligation to, 31, 32, 33.
*Sacerdos supplens,* see substitute.
Salary,
loss of, 46, 47.
deprivation of, 53.
must be handed over to Ordinary, when absence is unlawful, 54.
Substitute,
appointment of, 42, 43.
his power to assist at marriages, 43.
Study, as cause for absence, 12, 13.
Superintendent of schools, should not be pastor, 42.
*Tempus utile,* 66.
Time of absence,
computation of, 45, 46.
Trial for non-residence, 16, 17.
Urgent necessity, as cause for absence, 40, 41.
Utility to Church or State, as cause for absence, 42.
Vacations, 38.

## BIBLIOGRAPHICAL SKETCH

Peter Reilly was born April 23, 1908, in Drumard, County Longford, Ireland. He received his elementary education in Corratober National School, County Cavan, and his college education in St. Mary's Seminary, Moyne, County Cavan. His philosophical and theological studies were made in St. John's College, Waterford, where he was ordained June 12, 1932. In September, 1932, he entered the School of Canon Law at the Catholic University of America. From this institution he received the degrees J.C.B. in 1933 and J.C.L. in 1934.

## CANON LAW STUDIES

1. Freriks, Rev. Celestine A., C.PP.S., J.C.D., Religious Congregations in Their External Relations, 121 pp., 1916.
2. Galliher, Rev. Daniel M., O.P., J.C.D., Canonical Elections, 117 pp., 1917.
3. Borkowski, Rev. Aurelius L., O.F.M. De Confraternitatibus Ecclesiasticis, 136 pp., 1918.
4. Castillo, Rev. Cayo, J.C.D., Disertacion Historico-canonica sobre la Potestad del Cabildo en Sede Vacante o Impedida del Vicario Capitular, 99 pp., 1919 (1918).
5. Kubelbeck, Rev. William J., S.T.B., J.C.D., The Sacred Penitentiaria and Its Relations to Faculties of Ordinaries and Priests, 129 pp., 1918.
6. Petrovits, Rev. Joseph, J. C., S.T.D., J.C.D., The New Church Law on Matrimony, X-461 pp., 1919.
7. Hickey, Rev. John J., S.T.B., J.C.D., Irregularities and Simple Impediments in the New Code of Canon Law, 100 pp., 1920.
8. Klekotka, Rev. Peter J., S.T.B., J.C.D., Diocesan Consultors, 179 pp., 1920.
9. Wannenmacher, Rev. Francis, J.C.D., The Evidence in Ecclesiastical Procedure Affecting the Marriage Bond, 1920. (Not Printed.)
10. Golden, Rev. Henry Francis, J.C.D., Parochial Benefices in the New Code, IV-119 pp., (Printed 1925.)
11. Koudelka, Rev. Charles, J., J.C.D., Pastors, Their Rights and Duties According to the New Code of Canon Law, 211 pp., 1921.
12. Melo, Rev. Antonius, O.F.M., J.C.D., De Exemptione Regularium, X-188 pp., 1921.
13. Schaaf, Rev. Valentine Theodore, O.F.M., S.T.D., J.C.D., The Cloister X-180 pp., 1921.
14. Burke, Rev. Thomas Joseph, S.T.B., J.C.D., Competence in Ecclesiastical Tribunals, IV-117 pp., 1922.
15. Leech, Rev. George Leo, J.C.D., A Comparative Study of the Constitution "Apostolicae Sedis" and the "Codex Juris Canonici," 179 pp., 1922.
16. Motry, Rev. Hubert Louis, S.T.D., J.C.D., Diocesan Faculties According to the Code of Canon Law, II-167 pp., 1922.
17. Murphy, Rev. George Lawrence, J.C.D., Delinquencies and Penalties in the Administration and the Reception of the Sacraments, IV-121 pp., 1923.
18. O'Reilly, Rev. John Anthony, S.T.B., J.C.D., Ecclesiastical Sepultuae in the New Code of Canon Law, II-129 pp., 1923.
19. Michalicka, Rev. Wenceslas Cyrill, O.S.B., J.C.D., Judicial Procedure in Dismissal of Clerical Exempt Religious, 107 pp., 1923.

20. DARGIN, REV. EDWARD VINCENT, S.T.B., J.C.D., Reserved Cases According to the Code of Canon Law, IV-103 pp., 1924.
21. GODFREY, REV. JOHN A., S.T.B., J.C.D., The Right of Patronage According to the Code of Canon Law, 153 pp., 1924.
22. HAGEDORN, REV. FRANCIS EDWARD, J.C.D., General Legislation on Indulgences, II-154 pp., 1924.
23. KING, REV. JAMES IGNATIUS, J.C.D., The Administration of the Sacraments to Dying Non-Catholics, V-141 pp., 1924.
24. WINSLOW, REV. FRANCIS JOSEPH, A.F.M., J.C.D., Vicars and Prefects Apostolic, IV-149 pp., 1924.
25. CORREA, REV. JOSE SERVELION, S.T.L., J.C.D., La Potestad Legislativa de la Iglesia Católica, IV-127 pp., 1925.
26. DUGAN, REV. HENRY FRANCIS, M.A., J.C.D., The Judiciary Department of the Diocesan Curia, 87 pp., 1925.
27. KELLER, REV. CHARLES FREDERICK, S.T.D., J.C.D., Mass Stipends, 167 pp., 1925.
28. PASCHANG, REV. JOHN LINUS, J.C.D., The Sacramentals According to the Code of Canon Law, 129 pp., 1925.
29. PIONTEK, REV. CYRILLUS, O.F.M., S.T.B., J.C.D., De Indulto Exclaustrationis necnon Saecularizationis, XIII-289 pp., 1925.
30. KEARNEY, REV. RICHARD JOSEPH, S.T.B., J.C.D., Sponsors at Baptism According to the Code of Canon Law, IV-127 pp., 1925.
31. BARTLETT, REV. CHESTER JOSEPH, A.M., LL.B., J.C.D., The Tenure of Parochial Property in the United States of America, V-108 pp., 1926.
32. KILKER, REV. ADRIAN JEROME, J.C.D., Extreme Unction, V-425 pp., 1926
33. MCCORMICK, REV. ROBERT EMMETT, J.C.D., Confessors of Religious, VIII-266 pp., 1926.
34. MILLER, REV. NEWTON THOMAS, J.C.D., Founded Masses According to the Code of Canon Law, VII-93 pp., 1926.
35. ROELKER, REV. EDWARD G., S.T.D., J.C.D., Principles of Privilege According to the Code of Canon Law, XI-166 pp., 1926.
36. BAKALARCZYK, REV. RICHARDUS, M.I.C., J.U.D., De Novitiatu, VIII-208 pp., 1927.
37. PIZZUTI, REV. LAWRENCE, O.F.M., J.U.L., De Parochis Religiosis, 1927. (Not Printed.)
38. BLILEY, REV. NICHOLAS MARTIN, O.S.B., J.C.D., Altars According to the Code of Canon Law, XIX-132 pp., 1927.
39. BROWN, BRENDAN FRANCIS, A.B., LL.M., J.U.D., The Canonical Juristic Personality with Special Reference to its Status in the United States of America, V-212 pp., 1927.
40. CAVANAUGH, REV. WILLIAM THOMAS, C.P., J.U.D., The Reservation of the Blessed Sacrament, VIII-101 pp., 1927.
41. DOHENY, REV. WILLIAM J., C.S.C., A.B., J.U.D., Church Property: Modes of Acquisition, X-118, pp., 1927.

42. FELDHAUS, REV. ALOYSIUS H., C.PP.S., J.C.D., Oratories, IX-141 pp., 1927.
43. KELLY, REV. JAMES PATRICK, A.B., J.C.D., The Jurisdiction of the Simple Confessor, X-208 pp., 1927.
44. NEUBERGER, REV. NICHOLAS J., J.C.D., Canon 6 or the Relation of the Codex Juris Canonici to the Preceding Legislation, V-95 pp., 1927.
45. O'KEEFFE, REV. GERALD MICHAEL, J.C.D., Matrimonial Dispensations, Powers of Bishops, Priests, and Confessors, VIII-232 pp., 1927.
46. QUIGLEY, REV. JOSEPH, A.M., A.B., J.C.D., Condemned Societies, 139 pp., 1927.
47. ZAPLOTNIK, REV. IOANNES LEO, J.C.D., De Vicariis Foraneis, X-142 pp., 1927.
48. DUSKIE, REV. JOHN ALOYSIUS, A.B., J.C.D., The Canonical Status of the Orientals in the United States, VIII-196 pp., 1928.
49. HYLAND, REV. FRANCIS EDWARD, J.C.D., Excommunication, Its Nature, Historical Development and Effects, VIII-181 pp., 1928.
50. REINMANN, REV. GERALD JOSEPH, O.M.C., J.C.D., The Third Order Secular of Saint Francis, 201 pp., 1928.
51. SCHENK, REV. FRANCIS J., J.C.D., The Matrimonial Impediments of Mixed Religion and Disparity of Cult, XVI-318 pp., 1929.
52. COADY, REV. JOHN JOSEPH, S.T.D., J.U.D., A.M., The Appointment of Pastors, VIII-150 pp., 1929.
53. KAY, REV. THOMAS HENRY, J.C.D., Competence in Matrimonial Procedure, VIII-164 pp., 1929.
54. TURNER, REV. SIDNEY JOSEPH, C.P., J.U.D., The Vow of Poverty, XLIX-217 pp., 1929.
55. KEARNEY, REV. RAYMOND A., A.B., S.T.D., J.C.D., The Principles of Delegation, VII-149 pp., 1929.
56. CONRAN, REV. EDWARD JAMES, A.B., J.C.D., The Interdict, V-163 pp., 1930.
57. O'NEIL, REV. WILLIAM H., J.C.D., Papal Rescripts of Favor, VII-218 pp., 1930.
58. BASTNAGEL, REV. CLEMENT VINCENT, J.U.D., The Appointment of Parochial Adjutants and Assistants, XV-257 pp., 1930.
59. FERRY, REV. WILLIAM A., A.B., J.C.D., Stole Fees, X-107 pp., 1930.
60. COSTELLO, REV. JOHN MICHAEL, A.B., J.C.D., Domicile and Quasi-Domicile, VII-201 pp., 1930.
61. KREMER, REV. MICHAEL NICHOLAS, A.B., S.T.B., J.C.D., Church Support in the United States, VI-136 pp., 1930.
62. ANGULO, REV. LUIS, C.M., J.C.D., Legislación de la Iglesia sobre la intención en la applicación de la Santa Misa, VII-104 pp., 1931.
63. FREY, REV. WOLFGANG NORBERT, O.S.B., A.B., J.C.D., The Act of Religious Profession, VIII-174 pp., 1931.
64. ROBERTS, REV. JAMES BRENDAN, A.B., J.C.D., The Banns of Marriage, XIV-140 pp., 1931.
65. RYDER, REV. RAYMOND ALOYSIUS, A.B., J.C.D., Simony, IX-151 pp., 1931.

66. Campagna, Rev. Angelo, Ph.D., J.U.D., Il Vicario Generale del Vescovo, VII-205 pp., 1931.
67. Cox, Rev. Joseph Godfrey, A.B., J.C.D., The Administration of Seminaries, VI-124 pp., 1931.
68. Gregory, Rev. Donald J., J.U.D., The Pauline Privilege, XV-165 pp., 1931.
60. Donohue, Rev. John F., J.C.D., The Impediment of Crime, VIII-110 pp., 1931.
70. Dooley, Rev. Eugene A., O.M.I., J.C.D., Church Law on Sacred Relics, IX-143 pp., 1931.
71. Orth, Rev. Clement Raymond, O.M.C., J.C.D., The Approbation of Religious Institutes, 171 pp., 1931.
72. Pernicone, Rev. Joseph M., A.B., J.C.D., The Ecclesiastical Prohibition of Books, XII-267 pp., 1932.
73. Clinton, Rev. Connell, A.B., J.C.D., The Paschal Precept, IX-108 pp., 1932.
74. Donnelly, Rev. Francis B., A.M., S.T.L., J.C.D., The Diocesan Synod, VIII-125 pp., 1932.
75. Torrente, Rev. Camilo, C.M.F., J.C.D., Las Processiones Sagradas, V-145 pp., 1932.
76. Murphy, Rev. Edwin J., C.PP.S., J.C.D., Suspension Ex Informata Conscientia, XI-122 pp., 1932.
77. MacKenzie, Rev. Eric F., A.M., S.T.L., J.C.D., The Delict of Heresy in its Commission, Penalization, Absolution, VII-124 pp., 1932.
78. Lyons, Rev. Avitus E., S.T.B., J.C.D., The Collegiate Tribunal of First Instance, XI-147 pp., 1932.
79. Connolly, Rev. Thomas A., J.C.D., Appeals, XI-195 pp., 1932.
80. Sangmeister, Rev. Joseph V., A.B., J.C.D., Force and Fear as Precluding Matrimonial Consent, V-211 pp., 1932.
81. Jaeger, Rev. Leo A., A.B., J.C.D., The Administration of Vacant and Quasi-Vacant Episcopal Sees in the United States, IX-229 pp., 1932.
82. Rimlinger, Rev. Herbert T., J.C.D., Error Invalidating Matrimonial Consent, VII-79 pp., 1932.
83. Barrett, Rev. John D. M., S.S., J.C.D., Comparative Study of the Third Plenary Council and the Code, IX-221 pp., 1932.
84. Carberry, Rev. John J., Ph.D., S.T.D., J.C.D., The Juridical Form of Marriage, X-177 pp., 1934.
85. Dolan, Rev. John L., A.B., J.C.L., The Defensor Vinculi, XII-157 pp., 1934.
86. Hannan, Rev. Jerome D., A.M., S.T.D., LL.B., J.C.D., The Cannon Law of Wills, VI-517 pp., 1934.
87. Lemieux, Rev. Lelisle A., A.M., J.C.D., The Sentence in Ecclesiastical Proceduce, IX-131 pp., 1934.
88. O'Rourke, Rev. James J., A.B., J.C.D., Parish Registers, IX-109 pp., 1934.

89. Timlin, Rev. Bartholomew, O.F.M., A.M., J.C.D., Conditional Matrimonial Consent, X-381 pp., 1934.
90. Wahl, Rev. Francis X., A.B., J.C.D., The Matrimonial Impediments of Consanguinity and Affinity, VI-125 pp., 1934.
91. White, Rev. Robert J., A.B., LL.B., S.T.B., J.C.D., Canonical Ante-Nuptial Promise and the Civil Law, VI-152 pp., 1934.
92. Herrera, Rev. Anthony Parra, O.C.D., J.C.L., Legislacion Ecclesiastica sobre el Ayuno y la Abstinencia, 1935.
93. Reilly, Rev. Peter, J.C.L., Residence of Pastors, 1935.
    Cases of Evident Nullity, 1935.
94. Manning, Rev. John J., A.B., J.C.L., Presumption of Law in Matrimonial Procedure, 1935.
95. Moeder, Rev. John M., J.C.L., The Proper Bishop for Ordination and Dimissorial Letters, 1935.
96. O'Mara, Rev. William A., Canonical Causes for Matrimonial Dispensations, 1935.
97. Reilly, Rev. Peter, J.C.L., Residence of Pastors, 1935.
98. Smith, Rev. Mariner T., O.P., S.T.Lr., J.C.L., The Penal Law for Religious, 1935.
99. Whalen, Rev. Donald W., A.M., J.C.L., The Value of Testimonial Evidence in Matrimonial Procedure, 1935.

www.ingramcontent.com/pod-product-compliance
Lightning Source LLC
LaVergne TN
LVHW050157080826
844660LV00012B/308

* 9 7 8 0 8 1 3 2 2 2 8 6 8 *